ESCAPE

How to Have Victory
over Temptation

Stephen Chappell

First published in 2014 by Striving Together Publications, a ministry of Lancaster Baptist Church, Lancaster, CA 93535. Striving Together Publications is committed to providing tried, trusted, and proven books that will further equip local churches to carry out the Great Commission. Your comments and suggestions are valued.

Striving Together Publications
4020 E. Lancaster Blvd.
Lancaster, CA 93535
800.201.7748

Cover design by Andrew Jones
Layout by Craig Parker
Writing assistance by Lesley Rankin
Special thanks to our proofreaders

The author and publication team have put forth every effort to give proper credit to quotes and thoughts that are not original with the author. It is not our intent to claim originality with any quote or thought that could not readily be tied to an original source.

ISBN 978-1-59894-273-6
Printed in the United States of America

ACKNOWLEDGMENTS

Writing a book is never a solo endeavor. Many hands have been involved in this project, and I'm thankful for each of them. I'd especially like to thank Matt Chappell for providing great ideas in the formation stages of this project and Ryan Gass for his help with the devotional portion. Many thanks also to Lesley Rankin for her writing assistance and editing work.

Finally, special thanks goes to the Coastline Baptist Church family. Thank you for being a church family that embodies Hebrews 10:24–25 as you encourage one another in Christian growth: *"And let us consider one another to provoke unto love and to good works: Not forsaking the assembling of ourselves together, as the manner of some is; but exhorting one another: and so much the more, as ye see the day approaching."*

Contents

How to Use This Book

I write this book as a pastor who has a passion to help Christians
move beyond simply hearing the truth to personally applying
it to daily living. One of the most helpful ways to reinforce
the truths of God's Word is to give it entrance into our minds
in multiple ways—personally and with brothers and sisters
in Christ.

This book is written to include a variety of uses and is easily
adaptable for you to read alone or to work through its pages with
a group. It is presented in three sections—the book chapters, a
small group study guide, and a personal devotional. The study
guide and the devotions correspond with the chapters.

Whether you are a pastor looking for additional resources
for your church, a group leader planning a new series for Bible
study, or a believer just needing to know what God says about

temptation, I pray you'll find in these pages a valuable tool to enhance your spiritual growth and deepen your connections with your church family—brothers and sisters in Christ who, you will find as you study together, share the temptations and needs common to us all.

Below are suggestions to help you maximize the benefits of this book in its various uses.

Suggestions for Individual Study

- Read Part 1: How to Have Victory Through Temptation.

- Follow up with prayer and reflection in Part 3: Personal Devotions. These devotions correspond with each chapter of the book.

Suggestions for Group Study

Each of the six study guides in Part 2: Small Group Study Guide correspond with a similarly named chapter of the book. Each guide contains the primary Bible passage referenced in the chapter, a Lesson that reinforces three main principles of the chapter, several Focus Questions to prompt reflection and discussion, and a Challenge to encourage group members to apply their learning to their lives. This Bible study has been designed to take place over six weeks, but you are free to study at your own pace.

- Assign individual or group reading of each chapter of Part 1: How to Have Victory Through Temptation.

- Follow each chapter with a lesson from Part 2: Small Group Study Guide.

- Optional: Encourage group members to prepare for Bible Study in advance by completing the corresponding week of individual study in Part 3: Personal Devotions.

Suggestions for Study Group Leaders

- Don't skip the discussion questions. The discussion questions included in the Study Guide are key to engaging all members of your small group in the conversation. Most questions are practical rather than theoretical and can be answered through personal experience, which is a great tool for getting your group to open up and relate to each other on a deeper level. Use these and/or additional questions at your discretion to suit the specific needs of your group.

- Don't be afraid of awkward silences. Because many questions have a personal application, groups may be initially reluctant to share their thoughts or may need extra time to think about their answers. Be sure to share your own stories and experiences to help start the conversation and model answers for the group. Also consider posting questions a few days in advance of your Bible study through email or a Facebook group bulletin to give the group ample reflection time.

- Do create a comfortable environment for discussion. Whole-group discussion may not work best for your group. Many times people will feel more comfortable sharing personal experiences with one or two people rather than the entire group. Consider breaking out into smaller groups of two to four people for some questions. Keep tabs on these discussions, redirecting when necessary, and encourage groups to share key ideas from their discussions with the larger group.

- Do use the Focus Questions to your advantage. Many small group leaders find the Focus Questions can lead to discussions about outreach events or other initiatives the church family is planning throughout the calendar year. These questions are a great way to highlight the direction and vision of the local church, but a lengthy discussion may not be conducive to your study each week. To maximize your time, consider emphasizing just one or two Focus Questions or skipping this section when necessary to get right into the Lesson.

In whatever way you use this book, I challenge you to determine now—before you even begin the first chapter—to not just read or just discuss the biblical truths in these pages, but to actually apply them to your life. God has provided a way of escape for every temptation we face, but we must actually take the route He offers. May God bless you as you study and apply His truth.

1

How to Have Victory Through Temptation

I still remember my first day of first grade. I bounded out of bed almost before my mom could wake me and exchanged my cool Superman pajamas for my brand-new school clothes. In the bathroom I scrubbed my face clean with a washcloth, remembering to swipe behind my ears to pass the inspection my mom was sure to give. Then I hurriedly brushed my teeth and hair and dashed to the kitchen table to inhale some Cheerios so I could get to the best part of my day. I'd already met my teacher, Mrs. Krippoloni, and although she would be reading books and using colorful puppets like I remembered from Kindergarten, there was one big difference: first grade was officially "big kid" school.

I knew from watching my older siblings that there was a lot involved in going to "big kid" school. For one, I'd finally have more to put in my backpack than my lunchbox and favorite ball for recess. I would get assignments and projects that were a lot more involved than coloring a square and a triangle or circling whichever picture showed a puppy holding a particular letter of the alphabet. I was going to get real, actual homework!

Along with the homework, I also knew I was going to have some quizzes and (gasp) even a few tests. Of course, as an almost six-year old, I had very little understanding of what tests were, but I knew they existed and could be a little daunting. I knew they were things I had to pass to progress in my classwork and to advance from one grade to another.

As I grew, I became familiar with all sorts of different tests assessing my math skills, spelling and vocabulary knowledge (I always got extra preparation for these, since my mom was an English teacher), my recall of history facts, you name it, I was tested on it. And these tests came in a variety of formats, from multiple choice on the good ol' Scantron sheets with their formidable instructions that promised doom unless you used the exact type of No. 2 pencil, to the slightly more challenging fill-in-the-blank tests and the even harder essay exams (statistically, aren't you guaranteed a decent grade even if you choose C for every answer? Or is that just an urban legend?).

> Tests come in all different formats.

I came to learn that tests were just part and parcel of school life, and as long as I studied and did my best, chances were good I'd make it out alive. But when I didn't study and wasn't prepared…well, that was a different story.

I remember one particular test in high school—it was Chemistry or Biology, or some other subject ending in "y" that I just knew I'd never use in the real world—for which I thought I was ready, but after glancing over the first few questions, I realized I was wrong. You know that feeling of panic mixed with a little "I think I'm about to be sick" that you get after you've waited in a long checkout line at the grocery store and it's finally your turn and you realize you've left your wallet at home? Or when you step up to the podium to deliver a big speech and suddenly can't remember your opening lines? That's how I felt, staring at that test and realizing I was about to fail.

I began to wish frantically for a way out of taking that test. I didn't care how it happened—a campus-wide fire drill, a sudden case of twenty-four-hour stomach flu, an earthquake or some other natural disaster…hey, if Godzilla had suddenly rampaged through town and torn apart the ceiling of my classroom, I would've greeted him cheerfully. All I wanted in life at that particular moment was to escape.

Here's the thing: we don't stop having to take and pass tests when we leave school. Anyone who's lived a good deal of time knows our entire lives consist of tests—situations or opportunities to sin, or to become distracted from God's plan for us of obedience to and communion with Him. Some tests take the form of trials and difficult situations while others come as temptations, which can look different to each of us. For some, temptation looks like the urge to spend money you don't have for something you don't need. For others, it looks like the perfect opportunity to tell a lie or spread gossip. To one person, temptation is a decades-long struggle with substance abuse; for another person, it's a food or pornography addiction.

I've been saved for thirty-seven years now, and it didn't take me long in my Christian life to discover that being saved didn't mean I was never going to go through challenging times or never be tempted to do wrong. Temptation is just part of this adventure of being alive on earth. We could spend time asking why we have to deal with temptation, but the far better question is, "How can temptation be used in our lives?"

As a pastor, I've learned this question is immediately relevant and applicable to every single person, whether in my home church or in the body of Christ in general. And that's why I wrote this book. I want you to know God can use temptation to develop our character if we let Him. I want you to know the next time test day rolls around for you, it doesn't have to find you unprepared, frantically trying to recall the right answers and wishing desperately for a Godzilla-sized way out so you won't fail. When tests and temptation come calling, God already has an escape plan.

ONE

Dispelling the Myths about Temptation

When my sister was a little girl, one of our brothers had her convinced she was adopted. I'm not going to name names here (mostly because even after all these years he might still be able to take me if he really tried), but this brother would tease her about some strange little-girl habit or a random physical feature and say she'd gotten it from her "real" parents. If she'd misbehave, instead of just tattling, he'd threaten to have Mom and Dad send her back to her "real" family.

Don't get me wrong. Adoption is a beautiful gift—a special expression of love and chosen devotion. But when my sister was being teased that she was adopted because she didn't really fit in the family, that was a terrifying experience. When my sister tells the story now, she describes the very real anxiety she felt some nights, worried that our loving family was keeping such a dark secret from her.

I already know what you're thinking. "You mean she really fell for that? It's one of the oldest pranks in the book!"

I know, I know. All I can say in her defense is, she was an impressionable kid. Although deep down she knew it couldn't really be true, our brother had planted just enough doubt to make her wonder. Being older and (somewhat) wiser than she was, if anyone would know whether Mom and Dad had secretly adopted a baby to raise as a Chappell, it'd be our brother. And people were always saying how much my brothers and I looked like one or both of our parents, but hardly anyone said the same of my sister. Maybe these were signs! If she'd known about the Internet back then, I know her ten-year-old self would've been Googling "How to tell if you're adopted."

Of course, my sister eventually learned the truth. One day she made what she hoped was a casual mention of her adoption, and our mom laughed. "Of course you're not adopted," she said, as if my sister were quite possibly the silliest child she'd ever met. "Why would you ever believe that?"

My sister had no good answer. The idea just made sense at the time. But the truth made better sense, and what's more important, it put her fears to rest and gave her peace. She was a Chappell, really and truly. She belonged to these people we called *family*. What a relief it must have been to feel that weight slide off her shoulders!

Many times, what we think we know about a situation is more problematic than the situation itself. This is just as true of a little girl believing she'd been adopted as it is of each of us believing a myth about temptation. How can we hope to live victoriously in and for Christ if we believe temptation attacks us because we're horrible human beings or because God is mad at or wants to mess with us? How can we hope to overcome

> We'll never overcome temptation by relying on our own strength.

temptation if we think we have to rely on our own strength to do it—especially when it seems designed to target the weak spots in our armor?

There's something freeing and perspective-changing about learning the truth and dispelling a myth. In fact, that's one of the premises of the popular television show, *Mythbusters*. Once we know the truth, we can walk in it with confidence. And what better truth is there than what we find in God's Word?

One of the well-known Bible passages dealing with temptation is in 1 Corinthians 10. What's amazing to me is that the key to dispelling three of the most prominent myths about temptation is found in a single verse:

> *There hath no temptation taken you but such as is common to man: but God is faithful, who will not suffer you to be tempted above that ye are able; but will with the temptation also make a way to escape, that ye may be able to bear it.*—1 Corinthians 10:13

Myth #1:
"I'm being tempted because I did something wrong."

I can't tell you how many times I've heard some variation of this myth. It is beyond common for us to believe that trials and temptations come into our lives because we're weak or broken or guilty of some sin. Now don't get me wrong; when we fall to temptation, we *have* sinned. But too many people believe that the very presence of temptation indicates a problem. They think, "There must be something wrong with me because of the way I'm tempted."

One of the problems with this logic is that it's self-defeating. If I believe I'm only tempted because there's something inherently wrong with me, the battle's already half lost. Before long I'll lose the motivation to fight at all. I'll start thinking, "I don't have a chance of beating this, so what's the point of trying?" Soon I'll be giving way to temptation left and right and staggering under the weight of my own shame.

Truth:
Everybody gets tempted.

Here's the truth: there's nothing wrong with you. You are not the first to struggle with a temptation or set of temptations. Everybody—from the worst person to the "holiest" person you can think of—is tempted. We know this because in 1 Corinthians 10:13 Paul tells us temptation is *"common to man."*

While temptation is not common in the sense that we are all tempted by the same sin or trial, it is common in the sense that it happens to all of us, without fail.

Audience members of television talk shows will sometimes find themselves the lucky beneficiaries of gifts ranging from the useless to the extravagant, depending on the generosity of the show's producers. A comedian once joked that Oprah's audience gifts were so lavish they bordered on the ridiculous, like a personalized Rolls Royce. Little did he know that in 2007 for her annual "Favorite Things" episode, Oprah really would give everyone in the audience a brand new car.[1]

> Temptation is like a knife, that may either cut the meat or the throat of a man; it may be his food or his poison, his exercise or his destruction.
>
> —John Owen

Although temptation is certainly not a gift we want, it presents itself to all of us at various times in our lives. It doesn't come only to the rich because they have more resources to be tempted by. It doesn't come only to those who have made mistakes in the past because they're more likely to mess up again. Temptation happens to *everybody*.

It happened to Adam and Eve, the first people ever created. In Genesis 3:6 we read, *"And when the woman saw that the tree was good for food, and that is was pleasant to the eyes, and a tree to be desired to make one wise, she took of the fruit thereof, and did eat, and gave also unto her husband with her; and he did eat."*

Even Jesus experienced temptation (Luke 4:1–13; Hebrews 4:15). We'll talk more about this later, but one thing we can conclude is that if Jesus was tempted, the problem must not be with *being* tempted. It's not a sin to simply *be* tempted. The problem concerns how we respond to temptation.

Myth #2:
"I can't resist temptation."

Oscar Wilde famously once said, "I can resist everything except temptation," and sometimes this is the attitude we take when a test arrives in our lives. We give temptation too much credit in assuming it is inevitable that we will fall to it. Once I heard a woman complaining that she'd just ruined a weeks-long diet because a coworker had brought a plate of brownies to the office kitchen. When asked why she'd eaten them, she answered, "They just sat there, tempting me, taunting me, *daring* me. What was I supposed to do?"

Truth:
Temptation doesn't have to win.

If that lady had read our verse closely, she would have known what she was supposed to do. She was supposed to acknowledge the fact that she did have a choice. The first words are, *"There hath no temptation taken you."* The idea in the word translated *taken* means to be "overtaken." You see, while temptation may come, no temptation needs to overtake us. Succumbing to temptation is *not* inevitable.

If giving in to temptation were inevitable, there would be no need for the latter half of 1 Corinthians 10:13, which tells us that God provides a way of escape.

Myth #3:
"God won't give me more than I can handle."

Some Christians love to interpret 1 Corinthians 10:13 to mean, "God will never give us more than we can bear." I can understand why we would want to think this. It sounds great in difficult times, and sometimes it even brings a measure of comfort, however small. We think, "If God won't give me more than I can handle, He must have thought I was strong enough to handle this." The problem with this logic is that it puts the burden of getting through temptation and other difficult times squarely on us. But if God wanted us to handle our own problems, why would we have verses like these?

> *Casting all your care upon him; for he careth for you.*
> —1 Peter 5:7

> *Trust in the Lord with all thine heart; and lean not unto thine own understanding. In all thy ways acknowledge him, and he shall direct thy paths.*—Proverbs 3:5–6

God is our refuge and strength, a very present help in trouble.—PSALM 46:1

If anyone knew trouble in the Bible, it was David. In 1 Samuel 30—hunted by King Saul and on the run for his life—David's situation went from bad to much, much worse. He and his men returned from a trip to their encampment at Ziklag to find it burned and their wives and children taken captive. David's men, who had been loyal to him until that point, had finally had enough and were talking about killing him.

I'm sure some well-meaning person could've chosen that moment to commiserate with David, to pat him on the back and tell him, "Cheer up, buddy. God won't give you more than you can handle." But David didn't waste time trying to figure out whether or not he was strong enough to survive this latest trouble. He turned to his only source of help.

And David was greatly distressed; for the people spake of stoning him, because the soul of all the people was grieved, every man for his sons and for his daughters: **but David encouraged himself in the LORD his God.**
—1 SAMUEL 30:6

Truth:
God won't give you more than *He* can handle—and He can handle *everything*.

If you'll look back over the hardest times in your life you'll quickly find a pattern emerges: most of the things you thought you couldn't handle were things you *actually couldn't handle.* Not in your own strength, anyway. You see, God routinely gives us more than we can handle. And He does it with a purpose that leads back to Him.

Our society is consumed with the idea that we are in charge, that we should be our own heroes. The late Nelson Mandela, who was a hero to many, was said to be fond of the poem "Invictus" by William Ernest Henley. The last stanza reads,

It matters not how strait the gate,
How charged with punishments the scroll,
I am the master of my fate,
I am the captain of my soul.[2]

The thought that our "fate" is up to us is empowering, in a way. It makes us feel we can do anything. But here's the truth: if you're the captain of your soul, the only thing you'll do is cause a shipwreck. There is one story for all of human existence, and God is the author, the finisher, and the only hero of it. He is the only one capable of rescuing our souls from eternal spiritual death through salvation. Our victory over temptation and in life can only come as we realize our utter dependence on Him and His everlasting faithfulness to us. This is why Paul concluded in the latter half of our verse, "*...but God is faithful, who will not suffer you to be tempted above that ye are able; but will with the temptation also make a way to escape, that ye may be able to bear it*" (1 Corinthians 10:13).

Listen to these testimonies of our faithful God:

Know therefore that the LORD *thy God, he is God, the faithful God, which keepeth covenant and mercy with them that love him and keep his commandments to a thousand generations;*—DEUTERONOMY 7:9

It is of the LORD's *mercies that we are not consumed, because his compassions fail not. They are new every morning: great is thy faithfulness.*—LAMENTATIONS 3:22–23

The Lord knoweth how to deliver the godly out of temptations…—2 PETER 2:9

But the Lord is faithful, who shall stablish you, and keep you from evil.—2 THESSALONIANS 3:3

This realization should fill you with indescribable joy. God's power is so unimaginably great that He can save us from the pull of sin if we choose to yield to Him rather than to temptation. What's more, He keeps His Word—always. We read in 1 Thessalonians 5:24 that *"Faithful is he that calleth you, who also will do it."* But the key to knowing God's victory in life is knowing God personally as Lord and Saviour. The writer of Hebrews wrote, *"How shall we escape, if we neglect so great salvation…"* (Hebrews 2:3).

If we reject the offer of salvation made possible through Christ's sacrifice on the cross, we will never have the escape route we need to resist temptation and avoid sin and its resulting consequence—death (Romans 6:23). The only reason we even have the power to say "no" to temptation in the first place is because Jesus died to free us from our slavery to sin. The apostle Paul explained that before Christ, we were "the servants of sin" (Romans 6:17). This means we had no choice but to do wrong. Even the things we would think of as "righteousness" do not measure up to God's standard:

> For all have sinned, and come short of the glory of God;—ROMANS 3:23

> But we are all as an unclean thing, and all our righteousnesses are as filthy rags; and we all do fade as a leaf; and our iniquities, like the wind, have taken us away.—ISAIAH 64:6

The cross, however, makes possible a new way of life:

> But now being made free from sin, and become servants to God, ye have your fruit unto holiness, and the end everlasting life.—ROMANS 6:22

Do you know that you have a relationship with God? Do you personally know the faithful One who is our resource for victory over temptation and sin? If you do not or if you are not sure, I'd encourage you to turn right now to the Appendix of this book and read what the Bible says about how you can know.

If you do know Christ as Saviour, realize that He not only saved you from the penalty of sin—eternal separation in Hell—but He also saved you from the power of sin in your daily life. Because of what Jesus did at the cross, you and I have a way of escape from temptation.

1.   The Daily Beast Video, "Oprah's 5 Best Favorite Things Episodes," The Daily Beast, 2010, http://www.thedailybeast.com/articles/2010/11/19/moments-from-oprahs-favorite-things-giveaway.html, (accessed July 30, 2014).

2.   William Ernest Henley, "Invictus," Poetry Foundation, http://www.poetryfoundation.org/poem/182194#poem, (accessed July 30, 2014).

TWO

The Slow Slide

E ver seen a Chinese handcuff? Maybe you know it better by the name "Chinese Finger Trap" or "That joke your friend played on you that one time after asking, 'Wanna see something cool?'" The genius of this gag toy is its simplicity; it's just a small cylinder of woven bamboo strips. But when you place your fingers in the open ends of the cylinder and pull, the bamboo braid contracts, trapping your fingers inside. The more you pull, the more the trap tightens.

When I was growing up, I fell for this trick through a friend who loved practical jokes. He laughed and laughed as I struggled to free my fingers and when I became irritated with him, he shrugged. "Don't get mad at me—I didn't *make* you stick your fingers in it!"

Isn't that just how temptation works sometimes? We get ourselves in trouble when we willingly entertain it, and the trap closes around us the more we pull away from following God and the longer we allow temptation to stay in our lives unchecked. From there it just gets worse as we fall to sin and experience consequences that are sometimes far longer-reaching than we ever could have foreseen.

When it comes to temptation, a big problem rarely begins as a big problem.

A middle-aged man approached me recently and asked for spiritual counsel on an issue he was struggling with. He confided that his preoccupation with pornography had grown to addiction levels, something he was ashamed about but could not seem to overcome. I asked him how long he'd been dealing with this issue, and he told me it had been nearly thirty years.

You might wonder, "How is it possible for a Christian to struggle with a temptation like this for so long? How did things get so bad?" I'll tell you how: so slowly he almost didn't even notice it. His problem began when, as a boy, he was exposed to something he shouldn't have seen and *he didn't look away.* He willingly put himself in the trap. That choice led to another choice to see something else he shouldn't have seen, which led to even bigger choices with heavier consequences. All the while, he was moving further away from closeness with God, and the trap was tightening around him until one day he found the choice to look away hardly seemed up to him at all: he was addicted.

When it comes to temptation, a big problem rarely begins as a big problem. It begins as the song on the radio we should turn off, but ignore because we're too tired. It begins as the unedifying conversation at work that we don't partake in but remain part of long after we should've stepped away. It begins as that argument with a spouse that we leave unresolved just long enough to wonder if the grass isn't greener elsewhere. It begins with allowing ourselves to drive past a place we shouldn't frequent rather than taking an alternate route. On and on I could go, but you get the point. These are small decisions that we think are irrelevant at the time, but in hindsight we realize by making them we placed ourselves in the trap that led to sin.

None of this happens overnight. The man I mentioned earlier didn't wake up one morning with an addiction. You won't turn a corner tomorrow and discover you suddenly became an emotional overeater or have destructive anger issues. It's a slow slide into bondage.

Lot, Abraham's trouble-magnet of a nephew, can tell us something about the slow slide. It takes eight chapters of the book of Genesis (12–19) to tell his story. Let's take a look at his progression into temptation and sin.

The Backstory

Lot was the son of a man named Haran, who we better know as the brother of Abraham. When Haran died, Abraham took Lot in to raise as his own. We know from the Bible that Abraham was a man of great faith who loved God and sought to honor Him with his life. It was to Abraham that God said,

>   ...Get thee out of thy country, and from thy kindred, and
>   from thy father's house, unto a land that I will shew

thee: And I will make of thee a great nation, and I will
bless thee, and make thy name great; and thou shalt be
a blessing:—GENESIS 12:1–2

And God did bless him abundantly. The Bible says this future father of the Jewish nation *"was very rich in cattle, in silver, and in gold"* (Genesis 13:2). Surely, if there were a godly example to follow, it was Abraham's. Lot clearly benefited from his relationship with Abraham: Genesis 13:5 tells us *"And Lot also, which went with Abram, had flocks, and herds, and tents."* But a problem was brewing. Lot and Abraham had so many flocks and herds that it became hard to share the land between them, so they determined to go their separate ways.

And Abram said unto Lot, Let there be no strife, I pray
thee, between me and thee, and between my herdmen
and thy herdmen; for we be brethren. Is not the whole
land before thee? separate thyself, I pray thee, from me:
if thou wilt take the left hand, then I will go to the right;
or if thou depart to the right hand, then I will go to the
left.—GENESIS 13:8–9

The Slide Begins

What happened next in Lot's story was a decision that perhaps he looked back on with regret. At the time, however, it seemed harmless enough. Standing there with his uncle and being given his choice of the land that stretched before them on all sides, Lot did what many of us would've done in his place: he chose the land that would give him the greatest advantage.

The Bible says, *"And Lot lifted up his eyes, and beheld all the plain of Jordan, that it was well watered every where..."* (Genesis 13:10). For a man with lots of mouths to feed, this was an easy choice, right? Not so fast. The plain of Jordan had a major detraction: it was close to a city called Sodom, which was known above all else for its wickedness.

> *The men of Sodom were wicked and sinners before the LORD exceedingly.*—GENESIS 13:13

When Lot looked over toward the plain of Jordan, there's no doubt he saw Sodom in the distance. There's also little doubt he would have known of Sodom's widespread reputation. We don't have to ask what his response should have been. The Bible clearly says in 1 Thessalonians that we are to separate ourselves from even the appearance of sin (5:22). But like my friend with the pornography addiction, Lot's problem began because he didn't look away. Instead, he intentionally turned toward it.

> *Then Lot chose him all the plain of Jordan; and Lot journeyed east: and they separated themselves the one from the other...Lot dwelled in the cities of the plain, and pitched his tent toward Sodom.*—GENESIS 13:11–12

The Trap Tightens

Lot's slide began with his decision to look in the wrong direction, but he soon found just being close to the temptation represented by Sodom was not enough. Genesis 14 details the rebellion of the cities of the plain of Jordan, including the king of Sodom, against Elamite rule under King Chedorlaomer. When the rebellion was crushed, Chedorlaomer took goods and captives from those cities as his spoils of war. One name stands out among those captives.

> *And they took Lot, Abram's brother's son,* **who dwelt in**
> **Sodom,** *and his goods, and departed.*—GENESIS 14:12

Notice that by this time, Lot was no longer living just outside the sinful city of Sodom, gazing toward it from his tent. Now he was an official resident. We don't know how long he'd been living in the city, but we do know that he was already discovering there were some consequences of his choice. Lot had to be rescued by his uncle, who chased after Chedorlaomer's army with just 318 men, killed them all, and brought back everything and everyone that had been stolen (verses 13–16).

Just in case you think Lot learned his lesson, let's see how he's mentioned next in the book of Genesis. Chapter 19 opens this way:

> *And there came two angels to Sodom at even; and Lot*
> *sat in the gate of Sodom: and Lot seeing them rose up to*
> *meet them; and he bowed himself with his face toward*
> *the ground.*—GENESIS 19:1

So angels have come to visit the city and Lot is essentially rolling out the red carpet? This might be the opening of a pretty awesome story—until we consider why the angels happened to be in town. Genesis 18 tells us they'd just come from a visit with Abraham and that the Lord had told Abraham of His plan to destroy Sodom and Gomorrah because of their great wickedness. Knowing Lot lived in Sodom, Abraham pled for mercy, and God agreed to spare the cities if there were even ten righteous people living there (18:32).

Fast forward now to the angels' arrival in Sodom, and they don't have to look very far to find Lot: he was sitting right in the city gates. This is a significant detail because those who sat in the gates were typically important men, the political and business leaders of the city. Bible scholars have noted that the city gates were the center of community life: "In Eastern cities [the gate] is the market, the seat of justice, of social intercourse and amusement, especially a favorite lounge in the evenings, the arched roof affording a pleasant shade."[1]

So not only did Lot continue living in Sodom, but he allowed himself to be drawn closer into its wickedness. He was now a VIP of the city!

We can take Lot's situation as a caution that sometimes sin seems like it's actually paying off. If we're not careful, we can get to a point in our lives where we're not following God's will but there doesn't seem to be any negative consequences; in fact, it might seem as if we're thriving. Business is booming, we have money in our pockets, our relationships are going well, and there's nothing but sunny skies ahead. But don't be fooled: there is *always* a consequence for sin.

Be not deceived; God is not mocked: for whatsoever a
man soweth, that shall he also reap.—GALATIANS 6:7

Lot's sunny skies turned stormy very quickly after the angels' arrival. After an ugly run-in with the men of the city, the angels displayed God's power by blinding them and then telling Lot it was moving day. God had come to judge the city for its sin and anyone left there would be toast. Lot escaped with his wife and two daughters and a strict order from the angels not to look back. Tragically, his wife had trouble letting go, and she paid with her life.

But his wife looked back from behind him, and she
became a pillar of salt.—GENESIS 19:26

Amazingly, there's still more bad news to this story. After his escape, Lot had an incestuous relationship with his two daughters. The result was a set of grandsons who respectively grew up to establish the Moabite and Ammonite nations, which were enemies of the people of God. What a horrible slide! Lot went from being wealthy and blessed because of his association with Abraham, to having no wife, no home, no money, no VIP status, and having fathered some of the greatest enemies of God in the Bible—all because of his association with Sodom.

Lessons from the Slide

I wonder if, sometime in the days after fleeing Sodom, Lot didn't sit alone in his tent, maybe even catching a hint of smoke still in the air from the charred remnants of his old life, and wish wholeheartedly that he'd made a different choice all those years before when he stood beside Abraham surveying the land around them. If he had known the consequences of not looking away, perhaps the plains of Jordan with Sodom in the distance would not have seemed so tempting.

> We must intentionally turn away from sin, not toward it.

We don't know if Lot ever finally learned his lesson and made God-honoring choices with the rest of his life, but his is a cautionary tale for any of us who would entertain temptation. There are three lessons we can learn from Lot's slow slide if we'll pay attention.

Lesson #1: Protect your focus.

There's an old saying, "What you focus on becomes your reality," and this is so true of temptation. Remember, Lot's problem began when he didn't look away from sin. Soon, his reality was great wickedness and destruction. We can avoid the trap of temptation by focusing instead on the things of God.

> *Mine eyes are ever toward the LORD; for he shall pluck my feet out of the net.*—PSALM 25:15

> *Wherefore seeing we also are compassed about with so great a cloud of witnesses, let us lay aside every weight, and the sin which doth so easily beset us, and let us run with patience the race that is set before us, Looking unto*

*Jesus the author and finisher of our faith; who for the joy
that was set before him endured the cross, despising the
shame, and is set down at the right hand of the throne
of God.*—HEBREWS 12:1–2

Lesson #2: Pick your friends carefully.

Ever heard this one, "Show me your friends, and I'll tell you
who you are"? The people we pick to journey with us through
life have a profound impact on our character and behavior.
Remember that God agreed
not to destroy Sodom and
Gomorrah if there were only
ten righteous people, yet
only Lot and his daughters
were saved. Clearly, Lot had
few godly influences in his
life (apart from his uncle, who wisely kept his distance from
Sodom). This no doubt influenced his choices for the worse.
That's why Paul warned, *"Be not deceived: evil communications
corrupt good manners"* (1 Corinthians 15:33). If we want to avoid
the slow slide, we need to surround ourselves with people who
will encourage us to do right.

"Most people would
like to be delivered
from temptation but
would like it to keep in
touch."—Robert Orben

Lesson #3: Don't be greedy.

Greed is what motivated Lot's decision to make the plain of
Jordan his home in the first place. He already had abundant
wealth as God blessed him because of Abraham's faithfulness,

but he wanted more. Faced with the choice of which land to settle on, he literally picked the side where the grass was greenest. And we see how well that worked out for him.

Money is great—it helps put gas in our cars and food on the table, and every once in a while pays for a much-needed vacation. But with money also comes greater risk of temptation. Paul warned of this very concern.

> *But they that will be rich fall into temptation and a snare, and into many foolish and hurtful lusts, which drown men in destruction and perdition...Charge them that are rich in this world, that they be not highminded, nor trust in uncertain riches, but in the living God, who giveth us richly all things to enjoy; That they do good, that they be rich in good works, ready to distribute, willing to communicate.—*1 TIMOTHY 6:9, 17–18

Greed opens our hearts to the trap of temptation, but generosity and trust in God to provide for our needs is the way out.

Remember the Chinese handcuff from the beginning of this chapter? The key to freedom from that trap is counterintuitive; rather than pulling, you must push the ends of the cylinder toward the center in order to enlarge the opening and release your fingers. Freedom from temptation works much the same way. Rather than pulling further away from the God who wants to deliver us, we must push closer to Him and make following His will our priority. If we will look away from sin and keep our eyes on Him, we can avoid the slow slide and, unlike Lot, one day look back on our choices with no regrets.

1.   Robert Jamieson, Andrew Robert Fausset, and David Brown, *Commentary Critical and Explanatory on the Whole Bible* (Oak Harbor, WA: Logos Research Systems, Inc., 1997), 11.

THREE

The Greatest Escape Ever Told

I'm going to share with you what's probably one of the least profound insights you're going to read in this book: a pastor's life is hard. It's stressful. Sometimes it's so emotionally draining that I have no problem believing the statistic that fifty percent of new pastors don't make it five years in the ministry.

Now, don't get me wrong. I love this life and if God allows me, I will be pastor of Coastline Baptist Church until they wheel me away, old and feeble and just a little bit crazy (but in the fun way). But that doesn't mean that some days, being a pastor isn't one of the hardest things I've ever had to do. And while I have a wonderful wife and family who take care of me, I've had to learn that dealing with the pressures of ministry requires making the decision to take better care of myself. I've seen firsthand what happens to pastors who overdo it and are overcome by emotional strain and stress. So a while back, I decided to start improving my health by trying a workout that one of our associate pastors had been going on about. Perhaps you've heard of it—P90X? Yeah. That one.

All I knew about this workout was that it was pretty intense and gave amazing results. So I cleared out space in my garage, dusted off the gym equipment my wife and I had collected over the years, popped the first DVD into the machine and ran through some internal mantras to prepare mentally. (I'd like to tell you my mantra was something awesome like "Warrior mind, warrior fitness!" or "This is the first day of the rest of my life!" But it was more along the lines of "This is really gonna hurt in the morning.") The first night, I just watched as Tony Horton—this fitness machine with muscles down to his pinky toes—performed one of the most ridiculous workouts I'd ever seen. All I kept thinking was, "There's no way I can do this. This guy's out of his mind."

The next night I worked up the nerve to start trying a workout. And I was doing pretty good for a while. Tony and I were, well, if not on the same page, at least somewhere in the same book—until I reached about the twelve-minute mark of the workout. About that time I was drenched in sweat, my lungs wouldn't expand any more, my feet had a mind of their own, and I was convinced there was no way I was ever going to be a P90X warrior. Which meant I was never going to grow muscles down to my pinky toes. Which meant I'd cleaned out the garage for nothing. Which made me feel a little depressed and a lot tired, so I went in the house and sat on the sofa with a bag of popcorn and a Diet Dr. Pepper. Hey, don't judge me. Getting in shape is hard.

Here's how it all fits together. You may not know this, but no matter how hard I P90X'd, I was never going to be Tony Horton. In fact, some of the fitness models we see on television seem to exist just to prove we can never hit the mark to be like them. No matter how much product men buy, most will never get their hair to look just like the celebrities. No matter how much your teenage daughter diets and spends money on beauty tips, she'll never look like the airbrushed models on magazine covers, and chances are, your teenage son won't grow up to be the next Michael Jordan, no matter how many highlight reels and YouTube videos he watches (although Kobe Bryant does come pretty close—go Lakers!). This is because many times there's a secret behind how our models became who they are. Real people don't have the celebrities' hair budget, *Vogue*'s graphic design team, or Michael Jordan's personal trainers (or that insane vertical jump).

Of course, just because we'll never look or act *exactly* like our models doesn't stop us from trying. And in a way, it shouldn't stop us. Observing and following others' examples is how we learn. But we must be careful that the examples we follow are those that will point

> The examples we follow should point us toward God.

us toward God. In the last chapter we saw in Lot an example of a man who allowed himself to be trapped by temptation. This time we'll consider the example of One who made the greatest escape from temptation ever recorded—by relying on the Word of God.

The Temptation of Christ

We already mentioned in Chapter 1 that even Jesus was tempted. The writer of Hebrews revealed, *"For we have not an high priest which cannot be touched with the feeling of our infirmities; but was in all points tempted like as we are, yet without sin"* (4:15). Jesus experienced the trials and temptations that arise in our lives, with one crucial difference: He did not sin. This fact only gets more amazing when we realize that Jesus had to endure temptation much more intense than most of us ever will. On the occasion we'll study here, Jesus—recently baptized by John the Baptist in the Jordan River (Luke 3:21–22) and declared the Son of God before all who witnessed it—was ushered into the wilderness to face temptation from the devil. For forty days Jesus battled the world, the flesh, and Satan himself, who sought to distract Jesus from God the Father's divine plan for His life.

The account of Christ's temptation appears a few times in the Gospels (Matthew 4:1–11; Mark 1:12–13; Luke 4:1–13). There are several theories about why these accounts are not completely identical, but I think a lot can be said for the fact that writers have different styles and reasons for placing emphasis on certain things and not others. Matthew, for instance, was interested in recording Christ's life chronologically, while Mark was brief, wanting to emphasize this event in connection with Jesus's work of equipping His disciples. In Luke, we see the temptations Satan presented to Christ are not given in the order they happened. Rather, they are recorded in a way that corresponds to the order of temptations mentioned later in 1 John:

> *For all that is in the world, the lust of the flesh, and the lust of the eyes, and the pride of life, is not of the Father, but is of the world.*—1 JOHN 2:16

Let's see how Christ responded to each of these temptations in turn.

Temptation #1: Lust of the Flesh

Again, this temptation of Jesus was no momentary event. It went on for forty days. During that time Jesus had been fasting, so by the end of the forty days, He was understandably hungry. Can you imagine not eating for forty days? What would you pick as your first meal after breaking your fast? I'm pretty sure mine would be the biggest, juiciest steak I could find. But there was no steak in the wilderness—in fact, there was no food to be found anywhere. And so came the devil's first attempt to trap Jesus.

> *And the devil said unto him, If thou be the Son of God, command this stone that it be made bread.*—LUKE 4:3

There's nothing sinful about being hungry and wanting to eat; after all, food is a basic human need. The problem was in the priority. Satan wanted Jesus to put the needs of His body before the will of God. He wants to do the same to you, too.

Satan will try to use your flesh against you by convincing you that the desires of the flesh should come first. He'll say things like, "Do what feels good" or "The heart wants what it wants."

But Jesus had His answer ready. He quoted from Deuteronomy 8:3: *"And Jesus answered him, saying, It is written, That man shall not live by bread alone, but by every word of God"* (Luke 4:4).

Temptation #2: Lust of the Eyes

Undaunted, Satan moved on to the next temptation:

> *And the devil, taking him up into an high mountain, shewed unto him all the kingdoms of the world in a moment of time. And the devil said unto him, All this power will I give thee, and the glory of them: for that is delivered unto me; and to whomsoever I will I give it. If thou therefore wilt worship me, all shall be thine.*
> —LUKE 4:5–7

Essentially, Satan was saying, "Do you like what you see? It can be all yours right now." Who wouldn't have liked that view or the position of power Satan was offering? Satan was offering Jesus something that was already going to be His—in the Father's time. And implicit in this temptation was the offer to bypass the pain and humiliation of the cross.

Satan tries to undercut God's order in our lives in the same way, by offering things that many times are not wrong or sinful, but they bypass God's will and timing. He tells us, "Do you like what you see? Why wait when you can have it now?"

Again, Jesus had an answer from Scripture, this time from Deuteronomy 6:13:

And Jesus answered and said unto him, Get thee behind me, Satan: for it is written, Thou shalt worship the Lord thy God, and him only shalt thou serve.—LUKE 4:8

Temptation #3: Pride of Life

Even after two strikes, Satan keeps going. This time, however, he takes a page from Jesus' book and quotes Scripture (Psalm 91:11–12) to legitimize his words:

And he brought him to Jerusalem, and set him on a pinnacle of the temple, and said unto him, If thou be the Son of God, cast thyself down from hence: For it is written, He shall give his angels charge over thee, to keep thee: And in their hands they shall bear thee up, lest at any time thou dash thy foot against a stone.
—LUKE 4:9–11

Here, Satan tried to pervert Jesus's trust in the Father by daring Him to demonstrate it publicly, creating a spectacle before the crowds that were gathered at the temple below. With this temptation Satan captured the essence of the struggle of our human nature against our desire to live for the honor and glory of God: pride. Pride is the root of all sin and the foothold of all temptation. And it always leads to a fall.

When pride cometh, then cometh shame: but with the lowly is wisdom.—PROVERBS 11:2

Only by pride cometh contention: but with the well advised is wisdom.—PROVERBS 13:10

Jesus's third use of Scripture (Deuteronomy 6:16) was doubly meaningful:

And Jesus answering said unto him, It is said, Thou shalt not tempt the Lord thy God.—LUKE 4:12

Not only was this an answer to the literal temptation to put God the Father to the test, but it was also an answer to the pride the temptation was designed to exploit. By allowing Scripture to answer for Him, Jesus was prioritizing God's Word over the desire to live for self.

> Pride is the root of all sin and the foothold of all temptation.

Three times the devil tempted Jesus to sin, and three times Jesus combatted temptation with the Word of God. One could argue that Christ's knowledge of the Scriptures and triumph over temptation were all but assured because He is God. But there are three other factors that contributed to His victory.

He Understood the Consequences

When you are tempted, how often do you stop and consider the consequences of yielding to sin? If we're honest, sometimes we avoid thinking about the consequences because we don't want to talk ourselves *out* of giving in to the temptation. But Jesus knew exactly what was on the line. He knew that accepting

Satan's offers meant His Father's will would not be accomplished, the plan He'd set in place to redeem you and me on the cross would go unfulfilled, and His purpose for coming to live among sinful men would be completely missed.

It's helpful for us to remember that although God is gracious and willing to restore us even after falling to temptation, sometimes the opportunities we miss by doing so are gone forever. Jesus was unwilling to miss an opportunity to fulfill God's purpose for His life. Can you say the same?

> Let a man be but in earnest in praying against a temptation as the tempter is in pressing it, and he needs not proceed by a surer measure.
> —Robert South

He Understood the Power of God's Word

We have no shortage of evidence in the Bible of the power of God's Word in our lives:

> *For the word of God is quick, and powerful, and sharper than any twoedged sword, piercing even to the dividing asunder of soul and spirit, and of the joints and marrow, and is a discerner of the thoughts and intents of the heart.*—HEBREWS 4:12

> *Wherewithal shall a young man cleanse his way? by taking heed thereto according to thy word.*—PSALM 119:9

For I am not ashamed of the gospel of Christ: for it is the power of God unto salvation to every one that believeth; to the Jew first, and also to the Greek.—ROMANS 1:16

All scripture is given by inspiration of God, and is profitable for doctrine, for reproof, for correction, for instruction in righteousness: That the man of God may be perfect, thoroughly furnished unto all good works.
—2 TIMOTHY 3:16–17

What a testimony it is that Jesus Christ the Son of God, King of kings and Lord of lords, with all the power to command Heaven and Earth, turned to Scripture as His resource in temptation! His example shows us that if we want victory over temptation, we too must look to the Word of God. Of course, we can only use God's Word to combat temptation if we have taken the time to learn it.

This book of the law shall not depart out of thy mouth; but thou shalt meditate therein day and night, that thou mayest observe to do according to all that is written therein: for then thou shalt make thy way prosperous, and then thou shalt have good success.—JOSHUA 1:8

He Understood the Connection to Service

When Jesus answered Satan's offer to give Him all the kingdoms of the Earth, He showed an understanding of the true nature of temptation. At its core, temptation is a call to serve something other than God. What's more, we serve whatever or whomever we worship. As Christians, we are called to worship God, and the only service that is worthwhile is that which is done for the Lord.

> *Give unto the LORD the glory due unto his name; worship the LORD in the beauty of holiness.*—PSALM 29:2

> *Thou shalt worship the Lord thy God, and him only shalt thou serve.*—LUKE 4:8B

A far contrast from the story of Lot, Christ's responses during temptation give us a pattern to follow if we want to escape temptation as He did. In fact, Peter tells us following after Christ should be the goal of every Christian:

> *For even hereunto were ye called: because Christ also suffered for us, leaving us an example, that ye should follow his steps.*—1 PETER 2:21

Just like I felt while watching Tony Horton breeze through the complicated P90X exercises that I would never be able to follow his example, some people look at Christ's life and feel they could never follow Him because Jesus was perfect, while we are anything but. Here's the good news: Jesus Christ was a real person with a real life who understood what it was really like to be us. And while He lived a perfect, sinless life that none of us could ever hope to imitate on our best days, because He made us, He can clue us in on the secret to being just like Him. We see it in Luke 4:14, after Jesus' time of temptation is over:

*And Jesus returned **in the power of the Spirit** into
Galilee: and there went out a fame of him through all
the region round about.*

We are incapable of following Christ's example without
His enabling. We have to invite Him to live His life through us.
That's the only way we can access the power of the Spirit that
strengthened Christ to see victory over temptation.

FOUR

It's Who You Know

L ife has a way of reminding us of our weaknesses. That's the only explanation I have for our tendency to get "taken down a peg or two" just when we're feeling confident. You know what I mean: the public tumble down the stairs on the very day you get a new job or a promotion, or giving a great speech only to find out that you did it with spinach in your front teeth.

In my case, the humbling often comes even when I'm not feeling particularly confident. Remember my sad tale about P90X? What I didn't tell you was that I eventually made it through an entire workout. (If you're cheering, get ready to stop.) After throwing up and crawling into bed directly afterward, I woke up the next morning and found that what people had been saying about this program was right on target: it produced instant results. My chief result was that I was suddenly unable to move my arms.

I'm not exaggerating when I say I could not lift either of my arms high enough to do any part of my usual morning routine. I couldn't brush my own teeth or hair. And the pain I'd felt after the workout the night before had gotten so intense I could barely stand it. After these plus a few more bad-news symptoms that you couldn't pay me to list in this book, I made my way to the hospital, where I was immediately admitted and diagnosed with what the doctor called *rhabdo*—a condition that is much less fun than the nickname implies. Essentially, what happens with *rhabdomyolysis* is that muscle tissue breaks down and gets released into the bloodstream, and its products can get lodged in places they don't belong, like my kidneys.

As if the workout hadn't already reminded me how weak I was, the result of my exertion was so much worse. It was a horrible, horrible experience. I was only hospitalized for a day, but it took weeks to get back to normal. And of course I was blessed to relive the whole thing every time a well-meaning person asked why I was feeling poorly. Imagine my embarrassment having to admit that I'd injured myself exercising. (The excuse, "Oh, it's just an athletic injury" worked pretty well until people heard it happened after my first workout.)

> Our acceptance in life is not based on how strong we are or how much we can do.

We are reminded in times of weakness—like at no other time—that we are not up to the task of doing certain things on our own like make it through a p90x workout. Or defeat temptation. This is why it's crucial that we know someone who is up to the task. For the Christian, that Someone is God.

The Apostle Peter definitely knew something about overestimating his strength and failing because of it. I think Peter was one of those guys whom everyone likes to know—a confident "let's get down to business" type of guy who was always ready for an adventure and would defend a friend to the death if he had to. In fact, when Jesus shared in Matthew 26 that He would soon be crucified and His disciples would abandon Him, Peter refused to believe.

Peter said unto him, Though I should die with thee, yet will I not deny thee.—MATTHEW 26:35A

Jesus warned Peter against this overconfidence in his strength:

Watch and pray, that ye enter not into temptation: the spirit indeed is willing, but the flesh is weak.
—MATTHEW 26:41

And, of course, we know that Jesus was right. Just a short time later, although Peter valiantly tried to keep Jesus from being arrested, he was denying he'd ever known Jesus at all (Matthew 26:69–74). When he realized what he'd done, the shame and embarrassment he felt was so great that Peter *"went out, and wept bitterly"* (Luke 22:62). Yet, through this experience Peter learned that his flesh alone was not capable of conquering temptation. He learned that our acceptance in life is not based on how strong we are or how much we can do; it's based on God's unmerited favor.

To the praise of the glory of his grace, wherein he hath made us accepted in the beloved.—EPHESIANS 1:6

Because of what he learned, Peter's second letter to the believers in the North Galatia region emphasized the importance of knowing God. One Bible commentator wrote,

The word *know* or *knowledge* is used at least thirteen times in this short epistle. The word does not mean a mere intellectual understanding of some truth, though that is included. It means a living participation in the truth in the sense that our Lord used it in John 17:3, *"And this is life eternal, that they might **know** thee the only true God, and Jesus Christ, whom thou hast sent"* (emphasis added).[1]

In the opening verses of his epistle, Peter gives three benefits of knowing the God who can help us escape temptation.

When We Know Him, We Have the Power of Salvation

Simon Peter, a servant and an apostle of Jesus Christ, to them that have obtained like precious faith with us through the righteousness of God and our Saviour Jesus Christ: Grace and peace be multiplied unto you through the knowledge of God, and of Jesus our Lord,
—2 PETER 1:1–2

I love hearing and reading stories of how people came to know Jesus as Saviour. There's nothing quite like it for reminding me of the goodness, mercy, and complete awesomeness of our God. Because we are all wonderfully different and unique, no two stories are exactly the same. Some people were drawn through God's grace to salvation as children or teenagers, and others were convicted of their need for a Saviour later in life, perhaps after years of trying to fill His place in their hearts by some other method. Some stories are nothing short of miraculous—people delivered from addictions or gang violence, others surviving serious health problems or accidents that should have killed them, and going on to realize God's love and then trusting in Him for salvation.

Every once in a while I'll hear from someone who makes this disclaimer before beginning: "My testimony's not all that interesting." Usually, that's a story from someone who, like me, was raised in a Christian home and was in church so often it almost seemed as if they lived in the building. (I often joke that I was raised on drugs: I was "drug" to church for every Sunday morning, Sunday night, and Wednesday night service.) I understand the heart of someone who would wish their story were more "interesting" even if only to feel that their life change after trusting Christ was more dramatic. But the truth is, every story of salvation is compelling, not because of who we are or where we came from, but because of who God is.

I wonder if those people who would describe their testimonies as "boring" really understand the work that God does when we place our faith in Him. Peter certainly understood it. He knew that Jesus saves us by giving us three things that we can only find in Him: the righteousness of God, the grace of God, and peace with God.

> *Therefore being justified by faith, we have peace with God through our Lord Jesus Christ: By whom also we have access by faith into this grace wherein we stand, and rejoice in hope of the glory of God.*—ROMANS 5:1–2

And once saved, Jesus doesn't leave us to manage the rest of our lives on our own. He continues to lead us by conforming us to the image of His righteousness, enabling us through His grace, and comforting us with His perfect peace through the storms that come our way. All this is made possible *"through the knowledge of God, and of Jesus our Lord."* What *"precious faith"* indeed!

When We Know Him, We Have Power to Live

Not only are we saved through knowledge of God, but we're also equipped to live the lives He's called us to.

> *According as his divine power hath given unto us all things that pertain unto life and godliness, through the knowledge of him that hath called us to glory and virtue:*—2 PETER 1:3

Do you remember when you were a kid and begged your parents for a certain toy or game? After all the excitement when you finally got it, maybe for Christmas or as a birthday gift, one of the biggest letdowns was ripping open the packaging only to find three little words printed on the assembly instructions: "Batteries Not Included."

I think we sometimes approach the Christian life with a "Batteries Not Included" or "Some Assembly Required" mindset. We trusted God for salvation, but we think we have to find contentment from somewhere else. We trusted Him for salvation, but maybe we have to order self-control online. We trusted Him for salvation, but we'll figure out a way to just live with our anger and bitterness. After all, it only affects our lives *some* of the time.

Listen: the moment you placed your faith in God, you received *"His divine power,"* which is capable of doing all things—and that includes providing a way for you to conquer temptation, no matter what it is. Paul wrote,

> And ye are complete in him, which is the head of all principality and power.—COLOSSIANS 2:10

We have all the batteries we need to live rich, God-honoring lives in Jesus Christ. What would your life look like if you started behaving as if you believed this?

When We Know Him, We Have Power in His Promises

What's the value of a promise? I think most would agree it depends on our relationship with the promise maker. We hardly expect complete strangers to keep their promises; they have little invested in the relationship. But when we know someone and grow to depend on them, we expect them to keep their word.

No person on earth knows us as well as God does. He knows every detail about our lives, down to the number of hairs on our heads (Luke 12:7). And we are called to grow in our knowledge of Him (2 Peter 3:18) as we journey through life. In His goodness, God has made promises in His Word that we can expect Him to keep.

> *Whereby are given unto us exceeding great and precious promises: that by these ye might be partakers of the divine nature, having escaped the corruption that is in the world through lust.*—2 PETER 1:4

What are some of these "*great and precious promises*"? For starters, God promised to forgive our sins and restore our right standing with Him:

> *If we confess our sins, he is faithful and just to forgive us our sins, and to cleanse us from all unrighteousness.* —1 JOHN 1:9

He promised to be with us and provide the help and strength we need to live for Him:

> *And the LORD, he it is that doth go before thee; he will be with thee, he will not fail thee, neither forsake thee: fear not, neither be dismayed.*—DEUTERONOMY 31:8

And I will pray the Father, and he shall give you another Comforter, that he may abide with you for ever;— JOHN 14:16

Fear thou not; for I am with thee: be not dismayed; for I am thy God: I will strengthen thee; yea, I will help thee; yea, I will uphold thee with the right hand of my righteousness.— ISAIAH 41:10

I will instruct thee and teach thee in the way which thou shalt go: I will guide thee with mine eye.— PSALM 32:8

He promised wisdom to discern His will and peace regardless of the troubles we face:

If any of you lack wisdom, let him ask of God, that giveth to all men liberally, and upbraideth not; and it shall be given him.— JAMES 1:5

Be careful for nothing; but in every thing by prayer and supplication with thanksgiving let your requests be made known unto God. And the peace of God, which passeth all understanding, shall keep your hearts and minds through Christ Jesus.— PHILIPPIANS 4:6–7

Oh, and here's a promise that's especially relevant to our topic:

There hath no temptation taken you but such as is common to man: but God is faithful, **who will not suffer you to be tempted above that ye are able; but**

will with the temptation also make a way to escape,
that ye may be able to bear it.—1 CORINTHIANS 10:13

What a joy to know that we are not on our own when it comes to living the Christian life. God's *"great and precious"* promises cover everything we need to know. And He is the best promise maker of all, because He never fails.

Faithful is he that calleth you, who also will do it.
—1 THESSALONIANS 5:24

Know therefore that the LORD thy God, he is God, the faithful God, which keepeth covenant and mercy with them that love him and keep his commandments to a thousand generations;—DEUTERONOMY 7:9

Spiritual victory through God comes first as we enter into a relationship with Him through grace at salvation. But as Peter knew, victory in our daily lives comes only as we learn more and more about Him and understand what that relationship means. Knowing and growing in Jesus is the key to overcoming temptation and living fulfilled and joyful Christian lives.

---

1.   Warren W. Wiersbe, *The Bible Exposition Commentary.* (Wheaton, IL: Victor Books, 1996), 930.

No Happy Endings Here

My wife and I try to be intentional about having regular family times with our two daughters, and one of our favorite ways to hang out together has always been our family movie nights—complete with a bucket of popcorn and one of the most comfortable sofas you've ever stretched out on. More often than not our girls pick the movie, and when they were younger, that meant watching the same one over and over (And over. And over. And over.) They just couldn't get enough of their favorite stories.

Sometimes they'd get too excited or sleepy to sit through the entire movie, so they'd ask us to "skip to the good part," which was usually pretty near the end. Now I like to think I'm an observant guy, but some things—like children's movies—are kind of obvious. If you can count on anything in a kids' movie, it's no matter how different the plot details are—whether it's puppies that need to find their way home, a spunky orphan looking for some adoptive parents, or a princess that's missing a shoe—every movie ends the same way: happily (and with lots of music).

Well, when it comes to temptation, one writer was led of God to warn us of something that might not be so obvious: no matter how different the specific details are for each of us, when we yield to temptation, there are no happy endings. Not ever. In fact, as a character from one of my daughter's favorite movies is known for saying, "This can only end in tears."

I wish someone had shared that with me when I was a teenager. When I was sixteen years old, and shortly after I'd gotten my driver's license, I got the notion that it would be cool to take my dad's Buick LeSabre for an unapproved joyride while my parents were out of town for the weekend. My buddy Mitch came over, and we took the car out for a spin—literally. We hadn't gone five miles before I took a turn too sharply and hit a curb, skidded, and ended up blowing out two tires and wrecking the hubcaps.

I don't know which was worse: the agony of waiting for my parents to come home, knowing how much trouble I'd be in, or my dad's face when he saw what I'd done to his car. I can honestly say that night was one of the worst of my life. Not only were there plenty of tears involved, but it took me months of work to pay off my debt for the car repairs. If I'd only known the trouble I'd get into for just a few minutes of "fun" with my buddy, I'd never have picked up my dad's keys in the first place.

I wonder if that lesson is one of the reasons the book of James in the Bible was written for us. Some of the strongest and clearest words in the Bible on the topic of temptation are found in this book, and its focus is the destructive nature of sin. It's as if James is telling us, "If you knew how this story ends, you'd avoid sin like the plague it is."

Just a few verses into the first chapter of his letter, James gives a three-part warning about temptation that we would do well to remember.

God Will Never Tempt Us to Sin

James wrote, *"Let no man say when he is tempted, I am tempted of God: for God cannot be tempted with evil, neither tempteth he any man"* (James 1:13). The first thing to note about this verse is something we pointed out in Chapter 1 of this book, but it bears repeating: temptation is a fact of life. James did not say *"Let no man say if he is tempted,"* but *"when."* I doubt any of us can say, "I can't remember the last time I faced a temptation or trial," but even if that were true, it's only a matter of time before we're going to have another. Temptation is an inevitability.

But then James adds, *"Let no man say…I am tempted of God."* It might seem incredible that anyone could blame temptation on God, but humanity has been blaming God for our temptations and corresponding sin ever since the Garden of Eden.

*And the man said, The woman whom thou gavest
to be with me, she gave me of the tree, and I did eat.*
—GENESIS 3:12

So how are we to understand God's role in temptation? Remember, throughout this study we've been using the word *temptation* to include "testing" and "trial." And God does test us from time to time. In Genesis 22, for instance, He tested Abraham by asking him to sacrifice Isaac, his long-awaited and prayed-for son. But we must make a key difference between testing and temptation because God's testing will never entice us to sin. He will never send evil or harmful events into our lives. Instead, His tests are designed to benefit us by proving or strengthening our faith and producing character.

> God's tests are designed to help us, not hurt us.

*That the trial of your faith, being much more precious
than of gold that perisheth, though it be tried with fire,
might be found unto praise and honour and glory at the
appearing of Jesus Christ:*—1 PETER 1:7

That's how James could say earlier in Chapter 1, "*My brethren, count it all joy when ye fall into divers temptations*" (v. 2). He didn't mean that we should rejoice when we are tempted to sin; rather, that we should know God has our best interests in mind when He sends testing our way:

*Knowing this, that the trying of your faith worketh
patience. But let patience have her perfect work,*

that ye may be perfect and entire, wanting nothing.
—JAMES 1:3–4

Temptation Leads to Destruction

Have you ever wondered about the actual damage you can do to your tongue if you lick an icy flagpole? (You can pretend to not be curious, but when I Googled "What happens to your tongue…" it was the third result, so clearly the world wants to know.) Well, I know of one lady who found out firsthand. I'm not entirely sure how she got herself into the situation, but one thing is certain: her tongue was not the same afterward. She's still missing a chunk of it to this day.

When we head down the path of temptation, destruction is sure to come. That's what James meant by these words:

> *But every man is tempted, when he is drawn away of his own lust, and enticed. Then when lust hath conceived, it bringeth forth sin: and sin, when it is finished, bringeth forth death.*—JAMES 1:14–15

Here, James lays out a clear-cut formula: Lust leads to sin, and sin leads to death. This isn't the first connection in the Bible between sin and death:

> *For the wages of sin is death; but the gift of God is eternal life through Jesus Christ our Lord.*—ROMANS 6:23

In Romans, Paul is speaking of death as the eternal separation from God in the horrible place the Bible calls Hell.

Of course, if we have placed our faith in Christ, our salvation is eternal and irreversible (John 10:28–29). But that doesn't mean sin can't lead to a type of death—one in which we feel far from God, we have no joy, and we miss out on opportunities to be used of and bring glory to God.

We Don't Have to Take the Bait

Some of the greatest times of my life were times I got to spend with my granddad in Colorado's Rocky Mountains. He loved the outdoors, and he would often take me with him on fishing trips. I loved looking through his big tackle box to pick out which lures I'd use, and because he'd been fishing for much longer than I'd been alive, Granddad always knew which lures and what type of bait were guaranteed to trick the fish into thinking we had something good to offer.

Satan knows what type of bait is best to entice us, too. But unlike fishing, no matter how good the bait is, we don't have to bite it. We still have a choice about whether or not to sin, and that begins by recognizing the trap of sin for what it truly is.

James follows up with an interesting instruction:

Do not err, my beloved brethren. Every good gift and every perfect gift is from above, and cometh down from the Father of lights, with whom is no variableness, neither shadow of turning.—JAMES 1:16–17

His words *"Do not err"* seem to be oversimplifying our choice in temptation until we consider that the Greek word translated here as the phrase "Do not err" literally means "Don't be led astray." It cautions us not to err from the path of following God, and it implies that we need wisdom to recognize the tricks of the devil for what they actually are. It also reminds us, as we learned in Chapter 4, that we need to know some things about God. We need to know He is faithful and good and loving. Further, He wants us to realize that as His children we have the power in Him to overcome the lure of temptation.

We always have a choice about whether or not to sin.

Earlier I poked a bit of fun at children's movies because their happy endings are so predictable. But I have to admit that some of these movies are among my favorites, too. Sometimes on family movie nights, I'll have to pick between movies I've never seen before, and if anyone else has seen it, I'll ask "How does it end?" because when given a choice of what to watch, I'd much rather laugh than cry.

We don't have to wonder how the story will end if we yield to temptation. Through the inspiration of God, James has given us the perfect spoiler alert. The only question is, will you heed the warning?

The Courage to Hide

The story I've told countless times in the last seventeen years is still one of my favorites. It's the story of how God started Coastline Baptist Church, calling my family from a wonderful church home in Tennessee to an area of Southern California where we knew no one, and no one knew us. As anyone who has been involved with church planting can attest, it is not a journey for the fainthearted. I don't say that to boast about any exceptional bravery or heroism on the part of my family or myself. In fact, there have been plenty of times over the years when I've been so nervous about some aspect of this ministry that I just knew other people must be able to see my knees shaking. Being involved in a startup ministry is not a journey for the fainthearted because it requires us to do something we've heard and read about but so many times are afraid to do: completely depend on God.

It takes courage to trust the Lord. It takes courage to let go of the reins of our lives and allow ourselves to fall into His hands. But that's what we needed to do. We had to obey His calling on our lives and completely depend on Him to meet our needs.

Sometimes this was even harder than it sounds. I remember once in the very early days of Coastline when we believed it was God's will to reach our new community through a mailing. Sounds easy enough, right? How much trust could this require? Well, considering our bank balance at the time was hovering right at the $0.00 mark, that was a lot of trust. Another time, we arranged for Coastline to have its first guest speaker—another seemingly easy task, except for the fact that we had no money to offer as appreciation for the speaker's time, and although my family would be hosting him overnight, we had no food in the house. Again, we needed to trust God.

Hiding in the Word of God ensures our safety and expels our fear.

But one thing we find as we learn to lean on God is that He never disappoints. In the instance of the mailing, one day I received a phone call from a pastor I didn't know who had been asked by one of his neighbors (another person I didn't know) to give us $1,000. That money covered the cost of the mailing and then some. And when the guest speaker came, rather than having to apologize for not having any food in the house, God provided for that weekend and beyond. The man showed up in his Buick Roadmaster—

which, in case you're unfamiliar with it, is the largest car known to man—packed full of groceries for our entire family. Among the groceries was a case of microwave popcorn and a gallon of cooking oil that lasted for ages. I loved it because every time we opened the cupboard those items were a reminder of how God took care of us.

It's hard to trust God, particularly in times of trial and temptation. But it's even harder when you don't know what His Word says about the kind of God He is. It's even harder when you don't know what it says about His faithfulness, His great goodness, or His promises to meet our needs, fight our battles, and give us abundant lives as we follow Him. That's why we need to hide in the Word of God and hide the Word of God in us.

Sometimes we think of the concept of *hiding* as cowardly or inseparable from the feeling of fear. I remember playing hide and seek as a boy, and although there was a certain thrill in looking for the right hiding spot, I remember always being just a teensy bit afraid of being chased after and inevitably found. I knew it was only a game, but something about it also felt a little risky.

There's no risk at all in hiding in the Word of God. This is the sort of hiding that ensures safety and expels fear rather than causes it. Nothing will give us more clarity or direction in life than God's Word. In fact, everything we need to know to cover every aspect of our lives—including what to do when temptation arises—is found in its pages.

Psalm 119 is especially helpful when it comes to temptation. It is the longest of the Psalms, spanning 176 verses that are divided into sections of eight, with each section beginning with a letter of the Hebrew alphabet. It is a masterpiece of poetry and, with the exception of verses 122–123, each verse mentions the Word of God. It is in this psalm that we learn how to avoid sin from temptation, what to do when we are led to sin, and how to move on in a way that pleases God.

How to Avoid Sin

The opening lines of the psalm read,

> Blessed are the undefiled in the way, who walk in the law of the LORD. Blessed are they that keep his testimonies, and that seek him with the whole heart. They also do no iniquity: they walk in his ways.—PSALM 119:1–3

The idea is that a clean, "undefiled" life is connected to obeying God's Word and passionately seeking after Him. But how do we do that? We can't keep His law on our own, no matter how much we want to do what's right. The answer is His Word. We must spend consistent time in prayer and reading His Word to find the direction and enabling we need to follow Him. When we are committed to seeking Him this way, we'll find His instructions for life work every time.

> Victorious living does not mean freedom from temptation, nor does it mean freedom from mistakes.
> —E. Stanley Jones

Lead me in thy truth, and teach me: for thou art the God of my salvation; on thee do I wait all the day.
—PSALM 25:5

Sanctify them through thy truth: thy word is truth.
—JOHN 17:17

What to Do When We Sin

We've said it several times in this study, and hopefully it's sinking in that although every one of us has to deal with the reality of temptation, none of us is destined to succumb to it. In fact, we have a great God who has gone to great lengths to ensure that we have *"a way to escape"* (1 Corinthians 10:13). But none of us gets it right every time. That's why John wrote,

*My little children, these things write I unto you, that ye sin not. **And if any man sin**, we have an advocate with the Father, Jesus Christ the righteous:*—1 JOHN 2:1

So what do we do when we mess up? The answer is, we allow God's Word to get us cleaned up.

Wherewithal shall a young man cleanse his way? by taking heed thereto according to thy word.
—PSALM 119:9

The first step in understanding the power of God to cleanse us is realizing that through the saving work of Christ we can be free of the penalty of sin and assured of a home in Heaven.

*Purge me with hyssop, and I shall be clean: wash me,
and I shall be whiter than snow.*—PSALM 51:7

*So then faith cometh by hearing, and hearing by the
word of God.*—ROMANS 10:17

But if we will allow it, God's Word can lead Christians to a
spiritual cleansing from sin that restores us to a right relationship
with Him. Paul wrote the following to believers:

*Husbands, love your wives, even as Christ also loved
the church, and gave himself for it; That he might
sanctify and cleanse it with the washing of water by
the word, That he might present it to himself a glorious
church, not having spot, or wrinkle, or any such
thing; but that it should be holy and without blemish.*
—EPHESIANS 5:25–27

When we sin, we must remember that if we have placed our
faith in Him, we are forever accepted. We were granted God's
forgiveness for sin immediately at salvation. But recovery from
sin is accomplished through the power of the Word of God.

How to Move On

Not only does God's Word prepare us so we don't fall into sin
and cleanse us when we do, it fortifies us for future temptations.

The final verse we'll consider from Psalm 119 says, *"Thy word
have I hid in mine heart, that I might not sin against thee"* (v. 11).

The "*sin*" spoken of in this verse refers to temptation that hasn't yet arrived. We can trust God's Word to protect us now and in our future as we are faithful to hide it in our hearts, preserving it (through reading it, thinking on it, and memorizing it) for the next time we'll need it—because if there's one thing we can count on, it's that there will be a next time.

In late 2012, seventy-five-year-old Marion Shurtleff purchased a Bible in a used bookstore near her home in San Clemente, California. As she paged through it upon her return home she discovered a couple of folded pages tucked in the center of the Book. The yellowed sheets were covered with a child's handwriting that looked strangely familiar. To her amazement, Shurtleff discovered her own name at the top of the first page and realized the paper was an essay she'd written nearly sixty years before to earn a merit badge for her local Girl Scout troop—in Covington, Kentucky, more than 2,000 miles away.

How the Bible traveled that far is a mystery, but what I want you to notice is this: after all those years, this woman found her own story in a Bible. In a way, we each find our story in the Bible as well. No matter whether we're reading about Abraham and Lot, David, or Peter, or any number of the others who went before us, we can relate to their battles, failures, and victories. God recorded for us exactly what we need, if only we'll find the courage to hide His Word in our hearts and trust Him to deliver on His promises.

CONCLUSION

O ften when people come to me for counseling or advice, I find that after listening to their situation I'll offer some feedback or instruction, and they'll resist, saying something along the lines of, "Oh, but you don't really know what I'm going through."

Of course I don't know the situation of every person who is reading or ever will read this book. Like we've said several times, temptation can look differently for each of us. I'm only here to tell you what I know: regardless of what temptation looks like for you, if you've placed your faith in Jesus, you have an all-powerful God who died so you could live victoriously. And victory doesn't include falling prey to temptation every time it comes around.

In this book we've talked a lot about where to turn in times of trial and temptation. In the following pages you'll find even more encouragement in the form of small group Bible studies and personal devotions that will give you an opportunity to apply some of these principles directly to your life and your walk with Christ. Can I give you some pastoral advice now? All the help in the world is useless if you don't apply it in your life to the places where you need it most. So don't just read through these pages: really use them.

Let's take it even further. Although researchers recently disproved the notion that it takes 21–28 days to form a habit, what is certain is that habit is a matter of persistent and deliberate practice. The studies that follow are designed to be completed over six weeks, which is certainly long enough to establish a foundation for a lifelong pattern of depending on God's Word to find an escape in times of temptation. I challenge you to commit the next six weeks to growing in the knowledge of our Saviour and hiding more of His Word in your heart every day so that the next time temptation arises in your life, you'll be ready. Don't wait; start today. You'll be glad you did.

2

PART TWO

Small Group Study Guide

Dispelling the Myths about Temptation

Text

1 CORINTHIANS 10:6–13

6   Now these things were our examples, to the intent we should not lust after evil things, as they also lusted.

7   Neither be ye idolaters, as were some of them; as it is written, The people sat down to eat and drink, and rose up to play.

8   Neither let us commit fornication, as some of them committed, and fell in one day three and twenty thousand.

9   Neither let us tempt Christ, as some of them also tempted, and were destroyed of serpents.

10   Neither murmur ye, as some of them also murmured, and were destroyed of the destroyer.

11   Now all these things happened unto them for ensamples: and they are written for our admonition, upon whom the ends of the world are come.

12   Wherefore let him that thinketh he standeth take heed lest he fall.

13   There hath no temptation taken you but such as is common to man: but God is faithful, who will not suffer you to be tempted above that ye are able; but will with the temptation also make a way to escape, that ye may be able to bear it.

Introduction

Ever heard of test anxiety? Millions of students from college age to as young as third and fourth grade surely have. According to school psychologists, chronic test anxiety affects almost thirty percent of all students. Recorded symptoms range from worry, excessive studying, and sleeplessness the night before a test, to difficulty breathing or even passing out during a test. Not surprisingly for students, the higher the stakes of the test, the higher their anxiety and fear of failure.

While most adults have left behind for good the likelihood that advancing a grade or getting into college depends on a good exam score, there's no way to get through life without periodic tests. Many of these tests come in the form of temptations. While we may think temptations are designed for us to fail, if we consider some of the most common misconceptions about temptation in light of God's Word, we'll see the truth: with the right preparation and perspective, we can pass the tests of temptation with flying colors.

Discuss

- What is temptation? Why do we sometimes think being tempted is the result of wrongdoing?
- What are some of your first responses or reactions when you're faced with a temptation? (e.g., What questions do you ask of God? Who do you call? What music do you listen to? What does the temptation make you think about yourself?)
- Someone once said, "We usually know what we can do, but temptation shows us who we are." What does this mean?

Focus Questions

As we begin this study, consider the following questions:

- **Personal:** What does your typical response to temptation indicate about your relationship with God?
- **Community:** How can a misconception that temptation only happens to those who have done wrong hinder our relationships with others?
- **Worship:** How should the realization that we have a faithful God who prepares an escape during temptation impact our individual and corporate worship?
- **Mission:** How can we use the truth "God routinely gives us more than we can handle" as a tool to help unbelievers understand their need for a Saviour?

Lesson

1. **Succumbing to temptation is not inevitable.** Our responses to temptation can either move us forward or set us back, but the choice is up to us.

   A. **Observation:** First Corinthians 10:13 reads, *"There hath no temptation taken you…,"* and the idea in this word is similar to being "overtaken."

   B. **Interpretation:** Just because we are faced with temptation does not mean we have to step into it. We have a God who is willing and able to help us respond in the right way (Psalms 71:2; 141:10).

   C. **Application:** Have you ever felt "overtaken" or unable to resist a temptation? Be honest: what choice could you have made—even if it would've been difficult—to see a different outcome?

2. **Temptation is *not* unique to you.** We are all tempted, and Satan's temptation tactics have been the same since the beginning.

    A. **Observation:** Paul gave the Corinthians quite a list of sins to be on guard against in 1 Corinthians 10:6–10, and the implication is that these were some of the temptations most common to those living in the culture of the day.

    B. **Interpretation:** Temptations typically focus on one or more of three areas in all our lives: the lust of the flesh, the lust of the eyes, or the pride of life (1 John 2:16; Genesis 3:6).

    C. **Application:** Define the phrases *"the lust of the flesh," "the lust of the eyes,"* and *"the pride of life."* How are these applicable in areas with which you find yourself struggling?

3. **God's escape plan is not a way around temptation, but through it.** When we take on temptation in God's strength, we can emerge from it victorious and stronger for the experience.

    A. **Observation:** The second half of 1 Corinthians 10:13 reminds us, *"but **God is faithful**, who will not suffer you to be tempted above that ye are able; but will with the temptation also make a way to escape, that ye may be able to **bear** it."* Here, *bear* means "to endure, to stand up to or under."

B. **Interpretation:** While God does protect us from certain temptations (Matthew 26:41), He also gave us an example in Jesus of how to rely on Him through temptation (Hebrews 2:18; 4:15). We can count on Him to give us victory over temptation (2 Peter 2:9; Hebrews 2:3).

C. **Application:** Think of just a few ways God has shown Himself faithful to you throughout your life. How should knowing you can count on Him change your perspective and your response when temptation comes?

Challenge

As we'll see in the next studies, one of the best defenses against temptation is God's Word. Beginning today, start a list of memory verses to help you be victorious over the temptations that arise in your life. Some of the verses in the Personal Devotions sections of this book may be helpful in starting or adding to your list.

The Slow Slide

Text

GENESIS 13:2–13

2   *And Abram was very rich in cattle, in silver, and in gold.*

3   *And he went on his journeys from the south even to Bethel, unto the place where his tent had been at the beginning, between Bethel and Hai;*

4   *Unto the place of the altar, which he had made there at the first: and there Abram called on the name of the* LORD.

5   *And Lot also, which went with Abram, had flocks, and herds, and tents.*

6   *And the land was not able to bear them, that they might dwell together: for their substance was great, so that they could not dwell together.*

7   *And there was a strife between the herdmen of Abram's cattle and the herdmen of Lot's cattle: and the Canaanite and the Perizzite dwelled then in the land.*

8   *And Abram said unto Lot, Let there be no strife, I pray thee, between me and thee, and between my herdmen and thy herdmen; for we be brethren.*

9   *Is not the whole land before thee? separate thyself, I pray thee, from me: if thou wilt take the left hand, then I will go to the right; or if thou depart to the right hand, then I will go to the left.*

10   *And Lot lifted up his eyes, and beheld all the plain of Jordan, that it was well watered every where, before the* LORD *destroyed*

Sodom and Gomorrah, even as the garden of the LORD*, like the land of Egypt, as thou comest unto Zoar.*

11   *Then Lot chose him all the plain of Jordan; and Lot journeyed east: and they separated themselves the one from the other.*

12   *Abram dwelled in the land of Canaan, and Lot dwelled in the cities of the plain, and pitched his tent toward Sodom.*

13   *But the men of Sodom were wicked and sinners before the* LORD *exceedingly.*

Introduction

In 1948, Warner Bros. animator Chuck Jones introduced a pair of nemeses that would go on to battle each other for more than fifty years: Roadrunner and Wile E. Coyote, super genius. Cartoon enthusiasts will remember that no matter what strategy he employed, all the coyote's endless schemes to ensnare the roadrunner—some complicated and outright ludicrous and others deceptively simple—always backfired. Undaunted, the coyote would be back seconds later, ready to set another obvious trap for the roadrunner.

Often, we think temptation works just like the coyote did: complete with giant Acme Corporation boxes of complicated tricks and traps that we could clearly avoid if we really wanted to. But the truth is, temptation is much more subtle than the giant hole that suddenly appears in the path or the train track diverted to lead right off a cliff. We don't just suddenly fall into it. It's a slow slide.

Discuss

• Why is it so easy to "slide" into temptation? What are some of the signs along the way?

- How accurate is the excuse "the devil made me do it"?

Focus Questions

As we get into this study, consider the following questions:

- **Personal:** How can maintaining a close walk with God benefit us when it comes to making decisions about temptation?
- **Community:** How does our approach to temptation affect not only ourselves, but our families, our friends, and those we influence?
- **Worship:** What role does individual and corporate worship play in helping us honor God when making decisions about temptation?
- **Mission:** Why must we understand Satan's methods for tempting us if we are to be effective witnesses for Christ in our community and our world?

Lesson

1. **Stop the slide: protect your focus.** Refuse to be distracted for even one second by things that are not in line with God's Word and His will for your life.

    A. **Observation:** Lot did not begin his association with Sodom by buying a home there. Genesis 13:12 says he just *"pitched his tent toward"* this city that was already known for its wickedness (v. 13). But by Genesis 14:12, Lot was living in Sodom; and by Genesis 19:1, he was a leader of the city: *"And there came two angels to Sodom at even; and Lot sat in the gate of Sodom: and Lot seeing* *them rose up to meet them; and he bowed himself with his face toward the ground."*

B. Interpretation: If we keep our focus on the Lord, we will not be taken in by temptation (Psalm 25:15; Hebrews 12:1–2; Psalm 26:3).

C. Application: What things tend to distract you when you take your focus off God? What steps can you take to remind yourself where and how to refocus?

2. **Stop the slide: reconsider your companions.** Make sure the people you associate with are those who will help you make God-honoring decisions.

A. Observation: When Lot separated himself from Abraham, he gave up a godly influence in his life for the company of the citizens of Sodom, who *"were wicked and sinners before the LORD exceedingly"* (v. 13).

B. Interpretation: We take on the characteristics and habits of those with whom we spend the most time (1 Corinthians 15:33); thus, we should ensure we surround ourselves with people who encourage us to live for God rather than for ourselves (Psalm 81:12).

C. Application: What does your choice of friends say about your character?

3. **Stop the slide: don't be greedy.** A greedy heart is never satisfied and will always be susceptible to temptation.

A. **Observation:** Lot was already a wealthy man by the time he split from Abraham (Genesis 13:6), but still he wanted more. He took the best land for himself (vv. 10–11) and proceeded to climb the ranks in business and leadership once he was settled in Sodom (Genesis 19).

B. **Interpretation:** There are certain temptations connected to material wealth, and greed can make us prey to them (1 Timothy 6:9). Rather than finding security in possessions, we must be generous and look to bless others with what God has given us (1 Timothy 6:17–18).

C. **Application:** What do you do with the possessions and wealth God has given you? Do you try to grow your wealth just for the sake of having more? Or do you use what you have to help others?

Challenge

What temptations are you dealing with right now that may seem small but will grow to trap you in time? How can the steps above help you refocus and make the necessary adjustments to deal with these issues before they become larger problems?

The Greatest Escape Ever Told

Text

LUKE 4:1–14

1   And Jesus being full of the Holy Ghost returned from Jordan, and was led by the Spirit into the wilderness,

2   Being forty days tempted of the devil. And in those days he did eat nothing: and when they were ended, he afterward hungered.

3   And the devil said unto him, If thou be the Son of God, command this stone that it be made bread.

4   And Jesus answered him, saying, It is written, That man shall not live by bread alone, but by every word of God.

5   And the devil, taking him up into an high mountain, shewed unto him all the kingdoms of the world in a moment of time.

6   And the devil said unto him, All this power will I give thee, and the glory of them: for that is delivered unto me; and to whomsoever I will I give it.

7   If thou therefore wilt worship me, all shall be thine.

8   And Jesus answered and said unto him, Get thee behind me, Satan: for it is written, Thou shalt worship the Lord thy God, and him only shalt thou serve.

9   And he brought him to Jerusalem, and set him on a pinnacle of the temple, and said unto him, If thou be the Son of God, cast thyself down from hence:

10   For it is written, He shall give his angels charge over thee, to keep thee:

11   And in their hands they shall bear thee up, lest at any time thou dash thy foot against a stone.

12　And Jesus answering said unto him, It is said, Thou shalt not tempt the Lord thy God.

13　And when the devil had ended all the temptation, he departed from him for a season.

14　And Jesus returned in the power of the Spirit into Galilee: and there went out a fame of him through all the region round about.

Introduction

In 1961, social psychologist Albert Bandura conducted the first of his well-known "Bobo doll experiments," in which he measured children's responses after watching an adult behave aggressively toward a Bobo doll. The experiments demonstrated Bandura's social learning theory, which posited that one of the ways people learn most effectively is by watching others model a particular behavior or skill and observing the results.

Of course, the Bible was the premier authority on social learning long before Bandura's experiments. God's Word repeatedly warns us against harmful behaviors by showing us their consequences in the lives of others and exhorts us to godly living through the examples of those who accomplished amazing things through and for God (1 Corinthians 11:1). In our last study we saw the folly in allowing ourselves to slowly drift toward temptation in the example of Lot. In this study, we can be encouraged through the example of Christ, the ultimate role model, that when temptation comes we always have a ready answer in God's Word.

Discuss

- Name one role model in your life and briefly describe this person's influence on you.

- Why is it easier to learn from some examples and not others?
- In what ways does our success in life depend on our ability to learn from someone else's example?

Focus Questions

As we get into this study, think about your answers to the following questions:

- **Personal:** How often do you find yourself referring to God's Word, either through personal study or scripture memorization, in times of temptation?
- **Community:** How can becoming more familiar with Scripture help us better pray for and support our families, our friends, and others we influence?
- **Worship:** How does your worship reflect your understanding of God's protection and provision during temptation?
- **Mission:** Why must we know what it means to find reprieve in God's Word if we want to point others to Christ?

Lesson

1. **Understand the consequences of yielding to temptation.** We cannot redeem the past or make up for opportunities we miss by giving in to sin.

   A. **Observation:** Satan's first test was to appeal to Jesus' immediate physical need. Knowing Jesus was hungry, Satan said, *"If thou be the Son of God, command this stone that it be made bread"* (v. 3). But Jesus understood that taking this offer meant His Father's will would not be accomplished, and He would have missed His purpose.

B. **Interpretation:** While God is gracious and merciful to help us up after we fall (Proverbs 24:16; 1 John 1:9), if we fall to temptation we may forever lose certain opportunities and plans He had for us.

C. **Application:** What opportunities have you missed in the past because of sin? How is it helpful to understand what you might miss by yielding to temptation?

2. **Understand the power of God's Word.** We need to look no further than the Bible to find the power to resist the pull of temptation.

A. **Observation:** Each time Satan tempted Him, Jesus answered with a direct quote from Scripture (vv. 4, 8, 12). Clearly, He not only knew the Word, but He believed and obeyed it also.

B. **Interpretation:** If the Son of God thought it appropriate to answer temptation with His Word, how much more so should we rely on it to do the same? We must first know what the Bible says (Matthew 22:29), and then we'll find God will remind us of His Word when we need it most (Joshua 1:8; John 14:26).

C. **Application:** How well do you know your Bible, especially in relation to areas that are repeated points of temptation in your life? If you were tempted today in an area of weakness for you, would you have a biblical answer?

3. **Understand the connection between temptation and service.** Essentially, temptation is a call to serve ourselves. We have been called to serve Christ.

   A. **Observation:** When Satan tempted Him with all the power and glory of the world, Jesus answered, *"Get thee behind me, Satan: for it is written, Thou shalt worship the Lord thy God, and him only shalt thou serve"* (v. 8). He understood that we serve who or what we worship.

   B. **Interpretation:** We must remember that the purpose of our lives is to serve and worship God (Psalm 29:2). Anytime we are drawn away from a life of honoring God fully, that purpose is compromised.

   C. **Application:** How well do you understand your purpose? What things tend to distract or draw you away from that purpose? Who are you serving today?

Challenge

First Peter 2:21 instructs us to use Christ's life as an example: *"For even hereunto were ye called: because Christ also suffered for us, leaving us an example, that ye should follow his steps."* What is one practical way you can use His example of resisting temptation in your life this week?

It's Who You Know

Text

2 PETER 1:1–4

1   Simon Peter, a servant and an apostle of Jesus Christ, to them that have obtained like precious faith with us through the righteousness of God and our Saviour Jesus Christ:

2   Grace and peace be multiplied unto you through the knowledge of God, and of Jesus our Lord,

3   According as his divine power hath given unto us all things that pertain unto life and godliness, through the knowledge of him that hath called us to glory and virtue:

4   Whereby are given unto us exceeding great and precious promises: that by these ye might be partakers of the divine nature, having escaped the corruption that is in the world through lust.

Introduction

It's one of those sayings we've heard so often that no one remembers where it originated: *It's not what you know; it's who you know.* This phrase has been the foundation of advice to graduating college students and startup entrepreneurs for years. In fact, because researchers say 60–80 percent of jobs are found through personal relationships, some places like London's Cass Business School have actually employed a "professor of networking"[1] to teach students the importance of making strategic connections to bring social or financial advantage.

As Christians, our motive for establishing a relationship with God and other believers ought to be much less self-serving, but the principle is still the same: the better connected we are, the more we will flourish. As Peter learned through his experiences as a disciple of Christ, knowing Jesus and growing in Him is the key not only to escaping temptation, but also to receiving the power needed for a victorious Christian life.

Discuss

- How do our lives change as a result of knowing God?
- Why is it important to understand that if we have a relationship with God, we have complete acceptance in Him?

Focus Questions

As we get into this study, consider the following questions:

- **Personal:** How often do you find yourself trying to rely on yourself to conquer temptation? Why is this a mistake?
- **Community:** How should we function as members of the body of Christ in supporting each other and exhorting each other to behaviors that are pleasing to God?
- **Worship:** How should an understanding of our complete acceptance in Christ affect the way we worship?
- **Mission:** What would you say to someone who believes, "If nothing I can do will make God love me any less, what's the point of trying to live right?"

Lesson

1. **Knowing Him = Saving Power.** When we trust Christ for salvation we find unmerited and unending righteousness, grace, and peace.

   A. **Observation:** Peter writes that *"Grace and peace"* are *"multiplied"* to us *"through the knowledge of God, and of Jesus our Lord"* (v. 2). Before knowing Christ, the best we could do was offer our own righteousness, which cannot meet God's perfect standard (Isaiah 64:6; Romans 3:10). But with salvation, Christ extended His righteousness (Titus 3:5), His grace (Ephesians 2:8–9), and His peace (John 14:27).

   B. **Interpretation:** Too often we try to live in our own power, forgetting that Jesus didn't save us just to leave us on our own. The same divine power that saved us enables us to overcome temptation and be continually conformed to the image of Christ.

   C. **Application:** In what ways do you show a lack of trust in the saving power of Jesus by trying to live the Christian life on your own?

2. **Knowing Him = Complete Power.** When we know Him, we have complete access to the divine power that can save us from temptation.

   A. **Observation:** The gifts of salvation do not end with righteousness, grace, and peace. Peter continued,

> *"According as his divine power hath given unto us **all things that pertain unto life and godliness…**"* (v. 3).

B.   **Interpretation:** When we come to a saving knowledge of Christ, all the power we need in order to experience a victorious life is already included. We are *"complete in Him"* (Colossians 2:10).

C.   **Application:** If there's a lack of divine power in your Christian walk, it's not due to lack of availability. What steps do you need to take to better access the power of God in your life?

3.   **Knowing Him = Promising Power.** Through faith in God we become partakers in His promises, among which is that we will become more and more like Him.

A.   **Observation:** Peter adds that the *"glory and virtue"* (v. 3) we have been called to are possible through faith in God's *"exceeding great and precious promises: that by these ye might be partakers of the divine nature"* (v. 4).

B.   **Interpretation:** The power of God that saved us and equips us to live victoriously should also be working in us to make us look more and more like God, and less like the world (Romans 8:29; Romans 12:2).

C.   **Application:** How well does your life reflect the likeness of the God who created and saved you?

Challenge

Second Peter 3:18 tells us we should *"grow in grace, and in the knowledge of our Lord and Saviour Jesus Christ."* What are the telltale signs of someone who really knows Jesus? How well do you know Him? How are you seeking to know Him more?

---

1. Ian Jack, "It's not what you know, but who – the return of an unfortunate reality," The Guardian, June 29, 2012, http://www.theguardian.com/commentisfree/2012/jun/29/julia-hobsbawm-professor-networking-elitism, (accessed August 1, 2014).

No Happy Endings Here

Text

JAMES 1:13–18

13 *Let no man say when he is tempted, I am tempted of God: for God cannot be tempted with evil, neither tempteth he any man:*

14 *But every man is tempted, when he is drawn away of his own lust, and enticed.*

15 *Then when lust hath conceived, it bringeth forth sin: and sin, when it is finished, bringeth forth death.*

16 *Do not err, my beloved brethren.*

17 *Every good gift and every perfect gift is from above, and cometh down from the Father of lights, with whom is no variableness, neither shadow of turning.*

18 *Of his own will begat he us with the word of truth, that we should be a kind of firstfruits of his creatures.*

Introduction

It was a crime that had police shaking their heads. In August 2013, 46-year-old Thomas Langenbach was caught red-handed and convicted of burglary—of Legos. Over the course of a year, he'd stolen thousands of dollars worth of Legos from local Target stores by printing fake bar codes and buying the toys for steeply discounted prices. He then resold them on eBay and made about $30,000 in profit.[1]

Here's the head scratcher: Langenbach was employed as a vice president of a high-profile Silicon Valley software company and owned a $2 million home. With his executive salary and influence, he could have purchased all the Legos he wanted at bulk prices, become a legitimate online seller, and easily doubled his profit. Instead, he lost his job and his home, served time in prison, and will forever be known as the grown man who stole toys for less money than he made in a single month. Was it worth it?

Too often, we allow temptation to lure us away without considering the consequences of our choice. It's only later, when we are sitting on piles of broken dreams and missed opportunities, that we think, "If only I'd known it would end this way. If only someone had warned me, I'd have chosen differently." In His infinite goodness and grace to us, God included that warning in the book of James. If we are careful to heed it, we'll realize that knowing how temptation ends can help us escape, no matter how appealing the temptation may seem.

Discuss

- Think of a time you did something or were involved in a situation you regret. If you had realized all the consequences of your choice beforehand, how would you have approached the situation differently? Would you have weighed the risks more heavily?
- What's it like to watch your children, friends, or loved ones make choices you know will end badly? How does that experience give us a glimpse into the heart of God for His children?

Focus Questions

As we get into this study, think about your answers to the following questions:

- **Personal:** What is our responsibility as followers of Christ when it comes to being aware of the consequences of yielding to temptation?
- **Community:** How would you respond differently to temptation if you first considered its potential impact on your family, friends, and others around you?
- **Worship:** How is God glorified when we heed the warnings He's placed in His Word to keep us from temptation?
- **Mission:** How is God better able to use us as witnesses of the gospel message when we make a habit of considering the consequences of sin before we act?

Lesson

1. **Warning #1: Temptation is inevitable—and it's personal.** Each of us is guaranteed temptations that correspond to our personal weaknesses and areas of struggle

    A. **Observation:** James begins, *"Let no man say when he is tempted…"* (v. 13) and continues in verse 14, *"But every man is tempted…."* So the question is not *if* temptation will come, but *when* it will come. Additionally, the use of *man* and *he* instead of a general *we* or *us* indicates temptation can be specific to each of us.

    B. **Interpretation:** Just as we learned in our first study, temptation affects each of us, no matter what's in our

99

past or how long we've been following Christ. But it may not affect us the same way.

C. **Application:** Earlier in this chapter James wrote, *"My brethren, count it all joy when ye fall into divers temptations"* (v. 2). How can you find joy in the tests and temptations that arise in your life?

2. **Warning #2: The path of temptation leads to destruction.** Sin always draws us away from God and leads to a life of loss and regret.

A. **Observation:** James warns, *"But every man is tempted, when he is drawn away **of his own lust**, and enticed. Then when lust hath conceived, it bringeth forth sin: and **sin, when it is finished, bringeth forth death**"* (vv. 14–15).

B. **Interpretation:** For the Christian, the matter of spiritual death was already settled at the cross; however, sin will lead to guilt and a loss of joy, loss of our close walk with God, and loss of opportunities to bring glory to Him.

C. **Application:** James uses the word *enticed,* which gives the picture of being lured, baited, or tricked. How can viewing temptation as a master of deception help you understand your need for God's wisdom and warnings?

3. **Warning #3: Don't take the bait.** We have a choice when presented with temptation; we don't have to fall for it.

A. **Observation:** The word translated as *"Do not err"* in verse 16 means "don't be led astray; don't err from the path of following God." This indicates the choice is ours. But temptation will not be overcome by sheer willpower. James reminds us, *"Every good gift and every perfect gift is from above, and cometh down from the Father of lights, with whom is no variableness, neither shadow of turning. Of his own will begat he us with the word of truth, that we should be a kind of firstfruits of his creatures"* (vv. 17–18). Our relationship with Christ is what gives us the power for godly living and overcoming temptation.

B. **Interpretation:** Once we can recognize the tricks of temptation for what they are and where they lead, we can respond with the wisdom of Christ.

C. **Application:** How have you tried to combat temptation by your own willpower? What was the result? How did/would it be different if you relied on God's power?

Challenge

All of us are creatures of habit. If we want to make significant life changes, we must ensure they become part of our routine. What steps should you take if you want to develop the habit of dealing with temptation in the power of God?

1. Sebastian Murdock, "Thomas Langenbach, Lego Lover, Busted For Burglary Over Beloved Bricks," The Huffington Post, August 6, 2013, http://www.huffingtonpost.com/2013/08/06/lego-thief-langenbach_n_3715311.html, (accessed August 1, 2014).

The Courage to Hide

Text

PSALM 119:9–11

9   *Wherewithal shall a young man cleanse his way? by taking heed thereto according to thy word.*

10   *With my whole heart have I sought thee: O let me not wander from thy commandments.*

11   *Thy word have I hid in mine heart, that I might not sin against thee.*

Introduction

In the book *Beyond Belief: Finding the Strength to Come Back*, Josh Hamilton narrates his journey from success to a cycle of failures and back again. Once the #1 pick in the MLB draft and nicknamed the "Golden Boy" of baseball, Hamilton was sidelined by injuries sustained in a car accident in 2001 and became addicted to cocaine during his recovery. By 2005, he'd been suspended by the league for marijuana use and had been in and out of rehab clinics several times. He wrote, "I couldn't continue living the life of a crack addict, and I couldn't stop, either. It was a horrible downward spiral that I had to pull out of, or die. I was a bad husband and a bad father, and I had no relationship with God. Baseball wasn't even on my mind."

Realizing no amount of willpower or determination alone could help him change his life, Hamilton began spending long

hours in prayer and reading his Bible to restore his walk with
God. After a time of extended rehabilitation and additional
physical therapy, Hamilton was finally clean and sober and ready
to make a comeback to baseball. By 2008, he had set the record
for most home run hits in a round while playing for the Texas
Rangers, was a clubhouse leader with an impressive record, and
was awarded a Silver Slugger for batting excellence. When asked
about his success for an interview with ESPN, Hamilton said,
"How am I here? I can only shrug and say, 'It's a God thing.' It's
the only possible explanation."[1]

We all try to find a way to escape temptation that doesn't
involve trusting God and His Word. We claim to have faith, but
when it comes down to living by faith, we can struggle. But like
Hamilton, we won't see victory over temptation until we have
the courage to put our lives in His hands and hide ourselves in
His Word.

Discuss

- The verses describing the "armor of God" in Ephesians 6:10–20
  only include one offensive weapon: *"the sword of the Spirit,
  which is the word of God"* (v. 17). What does this suggest about
  how we should use the Bible in times of trial and temptation?
- What are five reasons you can think of for memorizing
  Scripture?

Focus Questions

As we get into this study, consider the following questions:

- **Personal:** How do you live by faith? What is your current practice for reading and memorizing the Word of God?

- **Community:** How does a deepened commitment to hiding in God's Word better prepare you to fulfill the roles to which He's called you at home, at work, and in the church?

- **Worship:** How does fully trusting in God's Word change the way we worship—not just singing or listening to sermons on Sunday morning, but the way we give, serve, and fulfill our purpose of bringing Him glory?

- **Mission:** How can your experiences learning to trust God and live by faith in temptation be used to bring others to a saving knowledge of Him?

Lesson

1. **God's Word purifies us from our past.** We are accepted in Christ through salvation, but recovery from sin is accomplished through the power of God's Word.

   A. **Observation:** The Psalmist writes, *"Wherewithal shall a young man **cleanse his way?** by taking heed thereto according to thy word"* (v. 9). The word *cleanse* speaks of washing off the dirt of sin (Psalm 51:7).

   B. **Interpretation:** Once we're saved, we are forever forgiven of sin and free from its penalty, but we all need to be regularly cleansed through God's Word from the effects of sin and temptation (Ephesians 5:25–27).

C. **Application:** What verses can you turn to when you need spiritual cleansing in your life?

2. **God's Word prepares us in our present.** Hiding His Word in our hearts will give us daily direction as we seek to live for Him.

    A. **Observation:** Verse 10 reads, *"With my whole heart have I sought thee: O let me not wander from thy commandments."* When we look to God through prayer and studying His Word, He will lead and direct us in the way we should go (Psalm 25:5; John 17:17).

    B. **Interpretation:** Looking to God for direction means acknowledging we cannot live the way we should on our own. We need to turn to Him with an attitude that acknowledges our inability and His complete ability.

    C. **Application:** In Psalm 25:5, David wrote, *"...for thou art the God of my salvation; on thee do I wait all the day."* Do you wait on God to direct you in daily decisions, or do you impatiently take the reins of your life, turning only to Him when you find yourself in trouble?

3. **God's Word protects us in our future.** Hiding His Word in our hearts will keep us from being drawn away by temptations that may be coming our way.

    A. **Observation:** In verse 11, the psalmist says, *"Thy word have I hid in my heart, that I **might not sin** against* *thee.*" This gives the idea of someone putting God's Word into safekeeping, a sort of "savings account" so it would be available in times of need.

B. **Interpretation:** Just like with our finances, a spiritual savings account stocked with God's promises is something many people don't think about building until they need it most. Don't be caught in a temptation without encouragement from God's Word to support and sustain you.

C. **Application:** How much of God's Word have you hidden away for emergencies? When's the last time you actively memorized or spent time thinking about Scripture?

Challenge

Take a look at the list below, "10 Practical Tips for Memorizing Scripture."[2] Try at least one of them this week.

10 Practical Tips for Memorizing Scripture

1. Memorize the Word of God in community.

With a small group or with the larger congregation, memorizing scripture as a community is a powerful way to learn the Bible together through pursuing mutual goals with accountability. Push each other to memorize the Word of God more. This is one way to live out Proverbs 27:17, *"Iron sharpeneth iron; so a man sharpeneth the countenance of his friend."*

2. Memorize along with your family.

Memory verses are not just for kids! If your children participate in programs that memorize Bible verses, invite the whole family to memorize together. This is a great way to teach the whole family the truth of the Bible.

3. Use note cards.

When you encounter a Bible verse you want to put to memory, make verse cards and place them in areas of your house or workplace that you will notice: on the bathroom mirror, in your living room, on your refrigerator, etc. Some people even memorize Scripture in the shower!

Deuteronomy 6:8–9 says we are to bind God's commands on our hands, on the doorposts of our houses and on our gates so that we can be constantly reminded of God and His commands. When we post verses all around our house we are able to more frequently meditate on God's Word, which helps us renew our minds.

4. Listen to an audio Bible.

Faith does come by hearing, right? A good way to redeem the time is to listen to Scripture while in the car, at the gym, or cooking. This is an ideal method for memorizing longer passages of Scripture and to set your mind on things above (Colossians 3:2).

5. Pray for God to help you.

Since God is the one who commands that we know Scripture and let it dwell in us, would He not answer a prayer to see His will done? Pray for help, guidance, understanding, and a deeper love for His Word.

> *Teach me, O LORD, the way of thy statutes; and I shall keep it unto the end.*—PSALM 119:33

> *Make me to go in the path of thy commandments; for therein do I delight.*—PSALM 119:35

> *Howbeit when he, the Spirit of truth, is come, he will guide you into all truth....*—JOHN 16:13

6. Study a passage of Scripture deeply.

When you pour over one portion of Scripture for days and weeks at a time, you can memorize a passage fairly easily. Reading the same set of verses over and over again will not only draw out riches from God's Word, but it will engrave those verses on your heart through repetition and deep meditation.

Suggested passages to start studying are Romans 8; Psalm 1; Ephesians 2:1–10; Ephesians 6:10–20; and John 3.

7. Find software to help.

Scripture Memory? There's an app for that! There are many websites and programs that can help you memorize Scriptures by providing plans and tools for your aid. Popular ones include MemVerse, RememberMe, and MobilizeFaith.

8. Put it to song.

Getting a song stuck in your head is another proof that music is a powerful tool to help memorization. That is why putting the Bible to song or listening to music filled with biblical lyrics is a useful way to internalize the Word of God.

9. Always be on the lookout.

During your normal study of Scripture or while you are listening to a sermon, be on the lookout for good verses to memorize. Having fresh Scriptures to meditate on will deepen your understanding of God and knowledge of Scripture.

10. Read out loud/write it out.

Reading out loud is a common tip for how to best memorize. It is one of the best memorization methods because it combines two learning styles: visual and auditory. Writing out the Scriptures is another way to memorize because it targets two learning styles as well: visual and tactile.

Other Tips

- Before you set to memorize a verse, read the passage the verse is from to make sure you know what it means in context.
- Don't forget to memorize the reference! This helps in your own personal study and for sharing with others.
- Think about how you can apply the verse to your life and pray for God's help in applying it.

- Use it or lose it! If you don't keep Scripture fresh in your mind, it may be easy to lose! Plan to review what you memorize from time to time to keep God's Word fresh in your life.

---

1. Josh Hamilton, "'I'm proof that hope is never lost,'" ESPN.com, July 5, 2007, http://sports.espn.go.com/mlb/news/story?id=2926447, (accessed August 1, 2014).

2. Edited from Kevin Halloran, "10 Practical Tips for Memorizing Scripture," www.unlockingthebible.org, https://www.unlockingthebible.org/how-to-memorize-scripture-bible-verses/, (accessed August 1, 2014).

3

Personal Devotions

1

DAY ONE

The Importance of Examples

Now all these things happened unto them for ensamples: and they are written for our admonition, upon whom the ends of the world are come.—1 CORINTHIANS 10:11

From trying a new recipe or health routine to finally building that set of shelves in the garage, we seldom approach new projects without a model or example to show us what we're aiming for. Examples help guide us, point out where we are lacking, and help us compare where we started to where we want to finish. Peter wrote that the Christian's greatest example is Christ: "*For even hereunto were ye called: because Christ also suffered for us, **leaving us an example, that ye should follow his steps***" (1 Peter 2:21).

What examples are you following for your life today? What sort of example is your life setting for others who are watching you?

Study Time

Read 1 Corinthians 10:6–10, and then answer the following questions in the space provided.

1. In verse 6–10, Paul gives a list of the temptations the Corinthians faced. If such a list were made for your life, what struggles would be on it?

_____

_____

_____

_____

2. What example(s) did the Corinthians have to help them resist these temptations (1 Corinthians 11:1)?

_____

_____

_____

3. What examples can you point to of people you know who have responded to temptation in the right way?

_____

_____

_____

Today's Prayer

God, You know everything about me. You already know the things that tempt me, and You have proven faithful to help me if I trust in You. Help me today to follow the examples You've provided for me and to trust You for victory over temptation.

Memorize 1 Corinthians 10:13 and 1 Peter 2:21.

2

DAY TWO
A Soft Heart

By humility and the fear of the LORD are riches, and honour, and life.—PROVERBS 22:4

The wrong perspective can be our downfall at any time, but it's especially dangerous in times of temptation. The Israelites learned this during the Exodus, when their stubborn and ungrateful hearts led them to complain about Moses' leadership, and God's provision for them because they had no water (Exodus 17:1–7). Pride, stubbornness, and ungratefulness lead to hardened hearts that are not likely to submit to God in times of temptation or to testify to the unsaved about His greatness. How's your heart?

Study Time

Read Psalm 95:6–10 and then answer the following questions in the space provided.

1. Why is humility important in the face of temptation?

_____

_____

_____

_____

2. In what ways have you shown a "hardened" heart in the past? What were some of the consequences?

_____

_____

_____

_____

3. What does it mean to "tempt" God? What effect does this have?

_____

_____

_____

_____

Today's Prayer

Lord, give me a soft heart that welcomes Your correction, guidance, and provision. Forgive me for times when I allow ungratefulness or doubt to lead me away from You.

One great cure for a hard heart is thankfulness. Make a list of ways God has shown provision for you just today. Thank Him for His great love for you.

3
DAY THREE
The Oldest Trick in the Book

Be sober, be vigilant; because your adversary the devil, as a roaring lion, walketh about, seeking whom he may devour:—1 PETER 5:8

Have you ever seen the game during which a magician passes a ball between cups, making it seem to appear and disappear at will? According to historians, this is one of the oldest known sleight-of-hand illusions in human history[1], yet street magicians still include it in their performances. Why? Because people still fall for it.

When it comes to temptation, Satan's been using the same trick since the Garden of Eden because Christians still fall for it. In God's strength we can be victorious over temptation, but often the first step is recognizing it for the trick it is and seeing Satan for who he really is—an enemy intent on destroying our lives and our testimonies for God.

Study Time

Read Genesis 3, and then answer the following questions in the space provided.

1. Describe three ways that the devil tempted Adam and Eve.

_____

_____

_____

_____

2. What is our natural tendency when we succumb to temptation?

_____

_____

_____

_____

3. How did God show grace to Adam and Eve despite their failure? How does He show grace to you when you fail?

_____

_____

_____

_____

Today's Prayer

Lord, teach me to recognize temptation when it comes, and show me the consequences of sin I may not see. Thank You for Your grace and forgiveness when I fall short. Help me to live for You in a greater way today than yesterday.

Memorize 1 Peter 5:8.

---

1. Matt Soniak, "What's the Oldest Trick in the Book?" Mental_Floss, March 3, 2014, http://mentalfloss.com/article/55202/whats-oldest-trick-book, (accessed July 30, 2014).

4
DAY FOUR
The Long Way Through

A man's heart deviseth his way: but the LORD *directeth his steps.*
—PROVERBS 16:9

California's Pacific Coast Highway is one of America's most famous scenic routes, stretching from San Diego to the North Coast. For a business trip or even a day excursion to San Francisco, the PCH is hardly the most expedient route. But travelers who invest extra time in making stops along the way for new experiences would be hard pressed to find a more perfect drive.

Just like a good road trip, sometimes we can best learn a life lesson when we stop looking for a quicker or easier shortcut and commit to taking the long way through. And when God is directing our journey, we'll find His route brings us closer to Him and makes our lives richer and more fulfilling.

Study Time

Read Exodus 13:17–18, and then answer the following questions in the space provided.

1. How is God's grace shown in verse 17?

_____

_____

_____

_____

2. When was a time that God led you down the longer route instead of the easiest route? What did you learn about Him through that journey?

_____

_____

_____

_____

Today's Prayer

God, help me to be thankful instead of irritated or doubtful when Your way seems long and Your reasons seem unclear. Help me instead to trust You and focus on what You want to show me about Yourself in these times.

5

DAY FIVE
Stand Still

What shall we then say to these things? If God be for us, who can be against us?—ROMANS 8:31

Oscar Wilde once wrote, "To do nothing at all is the most difficult thing in the world," and during times of trial or temptation this can be particularly true. It seems our natural tendency is to want to *do* everything we can to fix our situation in our own power. But often we need to learn—like the Israelites did in Exodus 14—that our best bet is to stand still. For the Christian, standing still is not "doing nothing." It is actively trusting God to show Himself strong and to do the work of deliverance that only He can do.

Study Time

Read Exodus 14:11–14, 18, and 31, and then answer the following questions in the space provided.

1. What temptation was Israel facing at this time?

_____

_____

_____

_____

2. What did God want to prove about Himself to both Israel and Egypt?

_____

_____

_____

_____

3. What part should "fear" play in our relationship with God?

_____

_____

_____

_____

Today's Prayer

Lord, teach me to trust in You instead of my own strength when I am tempted. Open my eyes to what You are proving about Yourself to me and those around me when I rely on You for deliverance.

6
DAY SIX
Bittersweet Memories

They shall abundantly utter the memory of thy great goodness, and shall sing of thy righteousness.—PSALM 145:7

Memory is tricky. Through dozens of experiments, scientists have demonstrated that not only are we notoriously bad at accurately remembering events the way they happened, we can be made to recall false memories with the right stimulation. This is because emotion plays a heavy role in memory—things we feel during an event can forever impact how we categorize and remember it. How important it is to recognize the goodness and grace of God in temptation! If we are careful to give Him thanks for His deliverance in our times of need, we will be more likely to look back on these times with joy rather than bitterness.

Study Time

Read Exodus 15:22–27, and answer the following questions in the space provided.

1. Why is bitterness especially dangerous in a season of temptation?

_____

_____

_____

_____

2. What does verse 27 tell you about the goodness of God?

_____

_____

_____

_____

3. What in your life needs to be given to God so He can turn
    bitterness into something sweet or sustainable?

_____

_____

_____

_____

Today's Prayer

*God, show me the things in my past I have held onto with bitterness.
Help me to recall how You were there to guide, protect, and provide
for me even if I did not realize it at the time. Give me a heart
of gratitude for the countless ways You show Your goodness to me
each day.*

What is one song that reminds you of God's goodness? Put
it on a playlist so you can remind yourself throughout the
day and week.

7
DAY SEVEN
Faith over Fear

The LORD is my light and my salvation; whom shall I fear?
the LORD is the strength of my life; of whom shall I be afraid?
—PSALM 27:1

According to the National Institute of Mental Health, more than six million Americans have been diagnosed with some sort of phobia. Far more people than have been officially diagnosed would admit to being almost irrationally afraid of something. And while the reported statistic is that more than 90% of the things we fear are completely insignificant, have already happened in the past, or will never happen, since the fall of man humans have been preoccupied with fear and worry.

The Bible is clear about where we are to turn when we are tempted to fear. Whether it's the account of David running from Saul, Daniel being sentenced to the lion's den, Elijah hiding in a cave from Jezebel, or Paul facing stoning for preaching the gospel, we see that our fears can be quieted through faith. When we trust the God who delivered our souls through salvation to fight our battles for us, we can rejoice no matter the outcome.

Study Time

Read Numbers 13:25–33, and then answer the following questions in the space provided.

1. What were Israel's fears about conquering the Promised Land?

_____

_____

_____

_____

2. How does fear keep us from seeing with eyes of faith?

_____

_____

_____

_____

3. What can you learn from Caleb's faith in the midst of the people's fearful speculation?

_____

_____

_____

_____

Today's Prayer

Lord, when I am afraid, remind me of the examples of Caleb, David, Daniel, Paul, and many others. Help me learn to turn to You instead of believing the voices of fear.

What are you afraid of? When are you most tempted to fear? Find five Bible verses that can help you remember to trust God instead of your fear.

1

DAY ONE
The Lure of the Dream

Let your conversation be without covetousness; and be content with such things as ye have: for he hath said, I will never leave thee, nor forsake thee.—HEBREWS 13:5

In 1931, James Truslow Adams coined the term *American dream,* defining it as an existence in which "life should be better and richer and fuller for everyone, with opportunity for each according to ability or achievement."[1] Although the term's meaning has shifted over the course of history, many still hold that living the American dream means achieving financial success and a high standard of living. And not coincidentally, surveys of American Christians over the years continue to reflect that two of the greatest areas of temptation are materialism and discontent.

There's nothing wrong with money or comfortable living. But when we live to get instead of give, we'll fall to temptation every time.

Study Time

Read Genesis 13:1–13, and then answer the following questions in the space provided.

1.   Abraham and Lot were both wealthy men. Why do you think it was Lot who struggled with prioritizing the wealth of the land rather than recognizing the pitfall it also represented?

_____

_____

_____

2. What does this passage teach us about temptation coming when life seems successful?

_____

_____

_____

3. In what ways are you like Lot when it comes to your possessions?

_____

_____

_____

Today's Prayer

God, help me keep my eyes and focus on You when I'm tempted to be discontent with all You've given me. Remind me that You are enough and all that I need.

Start today to cultivate a heart of generosity. Find a way to give away something God has given you to bless another person.

---

1. J.T. Adams, *The Epic of America* (San Antonio, TX: Simon Publications, 2001), 219.

2

DAY TWO
Trimming the Fat

Blessed is the man that walketh not in the counsel of the ungodly, nor standeth in the way of sinners, nor sitteth in the seat of the scornful. But his delight is in the law of the LORD; and in his law doth he meditate day and night.—PSALM 1:1–2

Want to lose weight and lower that cholesterol? Doctors have long said one sure way is to completely stop eating red meat and other foods high in saturated fat. But modest results can still be seen by trimming the fat on cuts of meat by just 20 percent. While some may believe trimming fat means losing flavor, others know the long-term health benefits far outweigh the temporary sacrifice.

Sometimes it's necessary to trim some metaphorical fat from our lives as well. Whether it's cutting down on excessive spending to reach a budget goal or separating ourselves from the bad influences of other people, we'll find that if God is guiding us, these short-term sacrifices will always reap long-term blessings.

Study Time
Read Genesis 13:10–18, and then answer the following questions in the space provided.

1. Why might Abraham have also been tempted to settle in the plain of Jordan?

_____

_____

_____

_____

2. What is the long-term blessing Abraham was promised for the sacrifice of separating from Lot and giving Lot the best, most productive land?

_____

_____

_____

3. What "fat" needs to be trimmed from your life? What negative influences do you need to separate from in order to improve your spiritual health and increase your resistance to temptation?

_____

_____

_____

Today's Prayer

Lord, show me the areas of my life that need trimming so I can better focus on You in times of temptation. Help me remember the sacrifice of these areas is nothing in comparison to Your provision and blessings in my life.

Memorize Psalm 1:1–2.

3

DAY THREE
In Good Hands

But God, who is rich in mercy, for his great love wherewith he loved us, Even when we were dead in sins, hath quickened us together with Christ, (by grace ye are saved;)—EPHESIANS 2:4–5

In 1993, skier Jeff Eckland was caught in an avalanche that broke his back and ribs and buried him under several feet of snow. He later told interviewers that in the almost seventeen minutes he was buried alive, a central thought that kept him from panic while waiting to be rescued was, "I'm helpless to save myself. But I'm in good hands."

Like Eckland, we are helpless to save ourselves from the certain death brought on by our sin and must trust in the rescue provided by Jesus's sacrifice on the cross. But our rescue doesn't end there. We must realize we are also helpless to save ourselves from the pitfalls of temptation in our daily lives. But if our faith is in Jesus, we're in the best hands of all.

Study Time

Read Genesis 14:8–16, and then answer the following questions in the space provided.

1. How does Abraham respond to Lot's need although Lot, who is now living in Sodom, does not deserve it?

   _____

   _____

_____

_____

2.   What does this passage teach us about God the Father?

_____

_____

_____

_____

3.   How should Lot have responded?

_____

_____

_____

_____

Today's Prayer

Lord, help me to remember when I am tempted that I am helpless to save myself and that You are willing and able to rescue me. Thank You for always being there to save me.

When's the last time you thanked God for rescuing you from a situation when you didn't deserve it? Take some time to do so now.

4
DAY FOUR
Who's in Your Corner?

My little children, these things I write unto you, that ye sin not. And if any man sin, we have an advocate with the Father, Jesus Christ the righteous.—1 JOHN 2:1

A July 2012 article in *Forbes* Magazine describes six people whose support is critical to achieve success: an Instigator (who motivates others toward success), a Cheerleader (the "biggest fan"), a Doubter (also called "the voice of reason"), a Taskmaster (provides the discipline to meet deadlines), a Connector (someone who's great at networking with others), and an Example (a mentor who's "been there, done that"). The article concludes, "With the right team, you can form a web of connections to make the seemingly impossible practically inevitable."[1]

While God has called us to serve Him in community, if we've placed our faith in Christ, we don't need a team of six to live out His purpose for our lives: we need the power of One. God's Spirit motivates us to do right, supports us with guidance and examples from His Word, and places the connections in our lives that we need to live abundantly for Him.

Do you have Him in your corner?

Study Time

Read Genesis 18:16–32, and answer the following questions in the space provided.

1. Why do you think God would "hide" from Abraham His intent to destroy Sodom and Gomorrah?

    _____

    _____

    _____

    _____

2. What do Abraham's continued questions (verses 24, 28, 30–32) suggest about our persistence in prayer?

    _____

    _____

    _____

    _____

3. Have you ever had someone in your life who prayed for you and looked out for you as Abraham did for Lot? How can you be that sort of advocate for someone else?

    _____

    _____

    _____

    _____

Today's Prayer

Lord, thank You for Your unfailing love and mercy that advocate for me when I sin. Help me to remember that everything I need for an abundant life, I already have in You.

---

1. Jessica Hagy, "The 6 People You Need in Your Corner," Forbes Magazine, July 17, 2012, http://www.forbes.com/sites/jessicahagy/2012/07/17/the-6-people-you-need-in-your-corner/, (accessed July 30, 2014).

5
DAY FIVE
Reminders of His Word

Keep my commandments, and live; and my law as the apple of thine eye. Bind them upon thy fingers, write them upon the table of thine heart.—PROVERBS 7:2–3

It is said that the reason tying a string around the index finger helps with memory is the nerves in those fingers have the quickest connections to the hippocampus, the part of the brain responsible for memory. A ribbon around the index finger is a constant pressure that works to activate those nerves and associate brain activity with a particular memory, keeping that pathway as a conduit for it.

Perhaps this is one reason the Bible is filled with instructions to *"tie"* or *"bind"* God's Word to our bodies (Numbers 15:38–39; Deuteronomy 6:8, 11:18; Proverbs 3:3, 6:21, 7:3)!

Study Time

Read Proverbs 6:20–23, and answer the following questions in the space provided.

1. Prior to a very sobering picture of what temptation can lead to, Solomon warns his son about the importance of *"thy father's commandment."* Why?

   _____

   _____

_____

_____

2.   How does God's Word "talk with us" when we're awake
     (v. 22)?

_____

_____

_____

_____

3.   How do we "bind" God's commandments to our hearts?

_____

_____

_____

_____

Today's Prayer

_Lord, help me to study and meditate on Your Word so that I can
know Your will for me and avoid sin when temptations arise._

Psalm 119:11 directly correlates hiding Scripture in our hearts
to avoiding sin: _"Thy word have I hid in mine heart, that I
might not sin against thee."_ What verse has been helpful to
you in a particular temptation you face? Memorize it today.

6

DAY SIX
Cutting New Teeth

Get wisdom, get understanding: forget it not; neither decline from the words of my mouth. Forsake her not, and she shall preserve thee: love her, and she shall keep thee.—PROVERBS 4:5–6

Humans' third molars have been called the "wisdom teeth" since around the seventeenth century because they appear between ages 17 and 25, when adolescents have matured into adulthood. The idea of becoming wiser with age fits with scientists' discoveries that the brain continues to develop until about age 25, but more importantly, it's corroborated in the Bible, where we read, *"With the ancient is wisdom; and in length of days understanding"* (Job 12:12). The Bible is clear that we are to seek and grow in God's wisdom if we want to successfully escape temptation and lead purposeful lives.

Have you cut your spiritual wisdom teeth yet?

Study Time
Read Proverbs 8:1–11, and answer the following questions in the space provided.

1. Why is wisdom *"crying out"* in verses 1–3, and who is she calling to?

_____

_____

_____

_____

2. What does this picture of wisdom reaching out tell us about
    what God desires for us?

_____

_____

_____

_____

3. How can wisdom protect you against sin?

_____

_____

_____

_____

Today's Prayer

God, I need Your wisdom today and every day if I am to live for
You. Help me to distinguish Your voice above all others when I
need direction.

James 1:5 says the key to getting God's wisdom is simple: ask
for it. When's the last time you did?

7
DAY SEVEN
The Power of Influence

Be not deceived: evil communications corrupt good manners.
—1 CORINTHIANS 15:33

Adults are quick to tell children and teenagers, "Pick your friends carefully," but we sometimes fail to take our own advice. Why would we think with age comes decreased need to be wise about the people with whom we surround ourselves? God knows the power of influence and how it can work for good or evil in all our lives, whether we are young or old. That's why Proverbs 13:20 warns, "*He that walketh with wise men shall be wise: but a companion of fools shall be destroyed.*" We must be careful to surround ourselves with companions such as those spoken of in Hebrews 10:24: "*And let us consider one another to provoke unto love and to good works.*"

Study Time

Read 1 Samuel 25:2–39, and answer the following questions in the space provided.

1. How did Abigail's influence make a difference in the conflict between David and Nabal? How would things have escalated if she had not intervened?

    _____

    _____

_____

_____

2. Abigail's name means "My father rejoices." How do we bring joy to our Father's heart when we walk in His wisdom?

_____

_____

_____

_____

3. How can we provoke someone else to do what's right?

_____

_____

_____

_____

Today's Prayer

Lord, purge me of those things and people in my life that would draw me away from You. Help me to surround myself with friends who want the things You want for me, and help me to be that kind of friend for others.

1
DAY ONE
The Price of the Easy Way

*Blessed is the man that endureth temptation: for when he is tried,
he shall receive the crown of life, which the Lord hath promised to
them that love him.*—JAMES 1:12

The story is told about Alexander Severus, Roman emperor
from 222 to 235 AD, whose assassination started the Crisis of the
Third Century. According to historians, when Germanic tribes
invaded the Roman Empire, Severus rallied his armies and
marched out to meet them in battle. When he drew near the
enemy, however, he decided instead to bribe them to retreat. The
troops, angered at Severus' decision to take an easy way out that
would make the Empire vulnerable in the long run, assassinated
their own leader not long afterward.

Warren Wiersbe observed Satan uses the same tactic with
temptation: "Satan wants us to sacrifice the eternal for the
temporary and take the 'easy way.'"[1] Don't be fooled. There's
always a price to pay when we trade what's right for what's easy.

Study Time

Read Luke 4:1–13, and answer the following questions in the
space provided.

1. Why do you think the devil tempted Jesus with hunger first? What does he tempt you with first?

_____

_____

_____

_____

2. Why is Scripture the most important weapon in fighting temptation?

_____

_____

_____

_____

3. What verses do you use to battle temptation in your life?

_____

_____

_____

_____

Today's Prayer

God, give me discernment and strength in times of temptation. Remind me through Your Word never to trade what's right for what's easy.

---

1. Warren W. Wiersbe, *The Bible Exposition Commentary* (Wheaton, IL: Victor Books, 1996), 183.

2

DAY TWO

Preparing for Battle

Put on the whole armour of God, that ye may be able to stand against the wiles of the devil.—EPHESIANS 6:11

While war is a controversial issue for many, few people would prefer to lose rather than win once they're already involved in a conflict. To this end, months—and sometimes years—before a shot is ever fired, heads of state strategically prepare for battle, studying the enemy, building public support, calling up reserve military and training troops, and increasing production of war resources.

Often, the biggest battles we'll face in life are within ourselves and against an enemy who wants to destroy us through sin. If we have a hope of winning this battle, we need a strategic plan. We need to learn our enemy's tactics and destroy his ability to attack through arming ourselves with a surefire defense system: the Word of God.

Study Time

Read Ephesians 6:10–18, and answer the following questions in the space provided.

1. According to Paul, what is the most essential piece of armor the Christian needs?

_____

_____

_____

_____

2. Where must our strength lie in times of adversity and temptation? Why?

_____

_____

_____

_____

3. Why do we need to be reminded that our battles and temptations are spiritual in nature?

_____

_____

_____

_____

Today's Prayer

Thank You, Lord, for giving me Your Word to be my preparation, protection, and provision in temptation. Help me be faithful to study and meditate on it so I won't be led into sin.

Make sure you're prepared for your next battle. Get a card small enough to fit in your wallet or on the sun visor in your car. On it, write out the top three verses that will help you overcome the temptation(s) you struggle with.

3

DAY THREE
Healing in His Hands

Bless the LORD, O my soul, and forget not all his benefits: Who forgiveth all thine iniquities; who healeth all thy diseases; Who redeemeth thy life from destruction; who crowneth thee with lovingkindness and tender mercies; Who satisfieth thy mouth with good things; so that thy youth is renewed like the eagle's.
—PSALM 103:2–5

Recently, a Canadian news organization profiled a man named Paddy Hughes, a self-proclaimed faith healer touring the country to cure conditions from headaches and asthma to angina. Hughes told the interviewer that although he doesn't quite know where his "power" comes from, people travel long distances to be touched by him when they can't find healing through other means. "When they have tried the rest," he said, "they come to me."

When Jesus healed people's physical and demonic diseases, He knew exactly where His power came from—the Father. And the results of His healing were both verifiable and miraculous.

Although God does not promise healing in this life from every physical malady, He is our Healer. In our times of fierce temptation or disappointing failure, He is the One to whom we can always turn for healing, refuge, and renewal. His power is real and life-changing, and He gives us healing through the powerful promises of His Word. Don't try to live a victorious life through any other means; you'll find everything you need in the Word of God.

Study Time

Read Matthew 21:12–17, and answer the following questions in the space provided.

1. Both times Jesus spoke in the temple, He quoted the Scriptures. Why?

_____

_____

_____

_____

2. What could take place once Jesus rid the temple of sin?

_____

_____

_____

_____

3. What should we learn by the response of those who were healed?

_____

_____

_____

_____

Today's Prayer

Lord, thank You for being the God who heals and redeems my life from destruction. Help me to trust You to see me through temptation, and give the glory and praise to You.

4

DAY FOUR
Help a Brother Out

But exhort one another daily, while it is called To day; lest any of you be hardened through the deceitfulness of sin.—HEBREWS 3:13

In a modern society that says our priority should always be to "Look out for Number One," the concept that we are responsible for and accountable to other people can seem foreign. But that's exactly what Christians are supposed to do. The Bible is clear that we are to watch out for each other. We must be sensitive to the temptations that others may be facing and, in love, encourage each other to do right.

Study Time

Read Romans 14:11–16, and answer the following questions in the space provided.

1. If we're not careful, how can we be a "*stumblingblock*" to other Christians (v. 13)?

   _____

   _____

   _____

   _____

2. How should we live with verse 11 in mind?

   _____

   _____

_____

_____

3. What do you do to exhort other believers? How can you do better?

_____

_____

_____

_____

Today's Prayer

God, help me be a better sibling to my brothers and sisters in the faith. Show me where my actions might be a stumblingblock for others, and keep me sensitive to Your leading so I can encourage those who need it.

Look in your contacts list or call your church office to get the name of someone in your church who could benefit from a little encouragement. Before the week is out, call, text, or email this person to arrange a visit or a coffee break.

5

DAY FIVE
The Spirit Knows

This I say then, Walk in the Spirit, and ye shall not fulfill the lust of the flesh.—GALATIANS 5:16

Although most Christians know about the Holy Spirit and are familiar with His work at Pentecost, not as many are aware of His role in the daily life of the believer. Jesus said the Holy Spirit was sent to "*guide you into all truth*" and "*shew you things to come*" (John 16:13). The moment we receive Christ, we are regenerated, indwelt, and sealed with the Holy Spirit. As a result, we have the potential to live lives of victory over sin. This potential is released by faith as we surrender control of our lives to Him.

Study Time

Read 1 Corinthians 2:9–12, and answer the following questions in the space provided.

1.   How are we able to understand and know God?

_____

_____

_____

_____

2. What do you think is "the spirit of the world" (v. 12), and how is it different from the Spirit of God?

_____

_____

_____

_____

3. What are you doing to deepen your understanding of God's Word?

_____

_____

_____

_____

Today's Prayer

God, show me more about You through the work of Your Spirit. Cause me to grow more in my understanding of You so I can live victoriously when it comes to temptation and sin.

6

DAY SIX
Redeemed to Be Holy

I am crucified with Christ: nevertheless I live; yet not I, but Christ liveth in me: and the life which I now live in the flesh I live by the faith of the Son of God, who loved me, and gave himself for me.
—GALATIANS 2:20

On the hit television show, "The Biggest Loser," contestants compete to see who can undergo the most dramatic weight loss transformation over a period of several weeks. Although nearly everyone who participates in the show ends up losing significant weight, it's no secret that many regain the weight after the show ends and they return home to their normal routines.

When it comes to sin, Peter was adamant that believers have no business returning to the way they lived before Christ, *"fashioning yourselves according to the former lusts in your ignorance"* (1 Peter 1:14). Rather, we are to be holy, like the One who redeemed us by His blood on the cross. And the life transformation that happens when we place our faith in Christ lasts much longer than a television season. It's lifelong.

Study Time

Read 1 Peter 1:14–19, and answer the following questions in the space provided.

1.   Why do you think Peter repeats himself when he says, *"be ye holy"* (vv. 15–16)?

   _____

   _____

   _____

   _____

2.   Why would we be tempted to return to our *"former lusts"* (v. 14)?

   _____

   _____

   _____

   _____

3.   How precious is the blood of Christ to you? When did you last thank Jesus for redeeming you through His death on the cross?

   _____

   _____

   _____

   _____

Today's Prayer

Thank You for the cross, Lord. Thank You for shedding Your blood to redeem my soul. May I show my gratitude by living the life You've called me to.

7
DAY SEVEN
Something to Talk About

Let the redeemed of the LORD say so, whom he hath redeemed from the hand of the enemy;—PSALM 107:2

It's one of the telltale signs that you love someone: you just can't stop thinking or talking about them. Everyone in your life knows all about this person—in fact, sometimes you'll go on and on about him or her until your friends are sick of listening.

When we enter into a relationship with Christ through salvation, everyone around us should know about it. It should be no secret that we are spending time in His Word, and growing to be more like Him every day.

Do the people in your life know of your love for God?

Study Time

Read Psalm 119:172–176, and answer the following questions in the space provided.

1. How can our tongues speak of God's Word?

_____

_____

_____

_____

2. Why could the psalmist say he did not forget God's commandments?

_____

_____

_____

_____

3. In what ways does your life praise the Lord for the gift of salvation (vv. 174–175)?

_____

_____

_____

_____

Today's Prayer

Lord, forgive me for keeping quiet about You when I should have been telling everyone around me about the great things You have done for me. Give me the boldness to share Your Word this week with someone who doesn't know You.

We all have people in our lives—at home, at work, at school, in the grocery store, or our favorite coffee shop—who don't know Christ. Ask God to give you an opportunity to share your love for Him with one of these people. When He does (and He will), don't let the opportunity pass you by.

1

DAY ONE
Who Is He?

I am the LORD, and there is none else, there is no God beside me: I girded thee, though thou hast not known me: That they may know from the rising of the sun, and from the west, that there is none beside me. I am the LORD, and there is none else.—ISAIAH 45:5–6

One of the longest-running television game shows is the Newlywed Game, in which three married couples are asked a series of progressively challenging questions to determine how well they know each other. In one version of the show, either the wives or husbands volunteered odd facts about themselves and whichever remaining contestant recognized the fact as belonging to their spouse had to yell, "That's my wife/That's my man!"

How well do you know your God? Do you recognize Him in the world around you? If you were tested on your knowledge of His character and works, would you pass?

Study Time

Read Matthew 8:23–27, and answer the following questions in the space provided.

1. If the disciples believed Jesus was Who He said, why do you think they asked themselves, "Who is this guy?" after Jesus calmed the storm (v. 27)?

_____

_____

_____

_____

2.   Why would Jesus, Who knew everything that would happen, still allow His disciples to get caught in a "tempest"?

_____

_____

_____

_____

3.   The disciples already knew Jesus could do amazing things (vv. 2–16). Why was it important for them to also know He controlled "the wind and the seas"?

_____

_____

_____

_____

Today's Prayer

Oh God, I want to know You more. Show me Yourself as I seek You in Your Word and in prayer this week.

Make a list of the things you know about God. Start with what you know about His character, then move to what you know about His miracles, what pleases and displeases Him, things He likes to do, etc. The longer your list grows, the more appreciation you'll have for Him and His work in your life.

2

DAY TWO
Semper Fidelis

It is of the LORD's mercies that we are not consumed, because his compassions fail not. They are new every morning: great is thy faithfulness.—LAMENTATIONS 3:22–23

Although its use dates back at least as far as the fourteenth century, Semper Fidelis is most commonly recognized by Americans as the motto of the United States Marine Corps. The phrase, which means "Always Faithful," was officially adopted as a motto in 1883 to signify the dedication and loyalty that Marines have to their duties, to each other, to the Corps, and to their country—even after leaving the service.

The commitment to be "always faithful" bonds Marines into a lifetime brotherhood, but God's commitment to us brings a relationship that lasts far longer. Before the world began, He knew His plans for each of us (Ephesians 1:4). He gave His life to reconcile sinful man to Himself, and He keeps and renews us daily through the promises of His Word. How great is His forever faithfulness to us!

Study Time

Read Luke 15:11–32, and answer the following questions in the space provided.

1. Why would the father have been fully within his rights to refuse to take his wayward son back?

_____

_____

_____

_____

2. What does this passage teach us our actions should be after we succumb to temptation?

_____

_____

_____

_____

3. Use examples from your life to illustrate how God's faithfulness, love, and grace far exceed anything we deserve?

_____

_____

_____

_____

Today's Prayer

Lord, Your faithfulness to me is so great I can barely comprehend it. Open my eyes and increase my understanding so I may better see the countless ways You are faithful to me every day.

3

DAY THREE
Never Failed Us Yet

Trust in him at all times; ye people, pour out your heart before him: God is a refuge for us. Selah.—PSALM 62:8

English composer Gavin Bryars was working on a 1971 documentary chronicling street life in London, when he became fascinated by a song sung by one of the homeless men being filmed. He recognized it as an old religious melody, "Jesus' Blood Never Failed Me Yet." When he returned home he arranged the song with original accompaniment and was amazed to see how the final recording impacted those who listened: "[They] were unnaturally subdued...a few were sitting alone, quietly weeping. They had been overcome by the old man's singing.... This convinced me of the emotional power of the music...that respected a tramp's nobility and simple faith."[1]

Oh, that we would be like that man who, although faced with trials and challenges of life, could impact countless others with a simple testimony: Jesus never fails.

Study Time

Read 1 Kings 19:1–18, and answer the following questions in the space provided.

1. Why was Elijah discouraged?

_____

_____

_____

_____

2. When Elijah heard from God, it was not in a great wind, an earthquake, or a fire, but "a still small voice" (v. 12). What is the significance of this?

_____

_____

_____

_____

3. Think of a time when you felt overwhelmed and helpless like Elijah. How did the Lord rescue you? What did you learn about Him in the process?

_____

_____

_____

_____

Today's Prayer

Lord, may my attitude and actions through the good times and the hard times of life point others to a God who is my refuge and strength and who will never fail me.

Memorize Psalm 62:8.

_____

1. John Schaefer, _New Sounds: A Listener's Guide to New Music_ (New York: Harper & Row, 1987), 59.

4
DAY FOUR
The Only Promises That Count

Faithful is he that calleth you, who also will do it.
—1 THESSALONIANS 5:24

Politicians are famous for making empty promises. Every election cycle, candidate after candidate tries to woo voters by making guarantees based on situations and a future that may never materialize; yet, these guarantees are many times an essential part of a successful political campaign. While voters realize many of the candidate's promises cannot possibly be kept, they vote on the hope that some will be.

When we place our faith in God, we have more than a dim hope that some of His promises will materialize. He teaches us by example that the only promises that count are the ones that are kept—and He keeps every one of His. Our trust is in a God who has never broken even one of His promises. "*God is not a man, that he should lie; neither the son of man, that he should repent: hath he said, and shall he not do it? or hath he spoken, and shall he not make it good?*" (Numbers 23:19).

What promises are you trusting God for today?

Study Time

Read Genesis 18:1–15, and answer the following questions in the space provided.

1. Why did Sarah laugh (v. 12)?

    _____

    _____

    _____

    _____

2. Why do you think God reminded Abraham in this passage about the promise He'd made years earlier?

    _____

    _____

    _____

    _____

3. Abraham and Sarah waited twenty-five years for God's promise to be fulfilled. What does this teach us?

    _____

    _____

    _____

    _____

Today's Prayer

God, I don't want to be led astray by emotion or faulty thinking when hardships arise. Remind me when I face temptation that I can rely on Your Word with perfect confidence.

Write down some of the promises of God that have been fulfilled in your life. The next time you face temptation, look at this list to remind yourself that He always keeps His Word.

5

DAY FIVE
When We Just Don't Get It

Bless the LORD, O my soul, and forget not all his benefits: Who forgiveth all thine iniquities; who healeth all thy diseases; Who redeemeth thy life from destruction; who crowneth thee with lovingkindness and tender mercies;—PSALM 103:2–4

Have you ever heard the phrase, "Learning the hard way"? Sometimes there are life lessons we have to be taught again and again before we truly understand. Jesus' disciples knew this. In the years they followed Him and helped Him minister to others, they repeatedly saw Him save, heal, and meet the needs of those who came to Him. Yet, there were still times they doubted His power. And we are no different. In fact, one Bible scholar wrote:

> God's people often have a tendency to forget His blessings. He meets our needs, but then when the next problem arises, we complain or become frightened. As long as we are with Him, we can be sure He will care for us. It would do us all good to pause occasionally and remind ourselves of His goodness and faithfulness.[1]

Study Time

Read Mark 8:1–21, and answer the following questions in the space provided.

1. Why were the disciples preoccupied in verses 14–16?

_____

_____

_____

_____

2. What two miracles had they just seen (vv. 5–9, 19–20)? How do you think Jesus felt about their forgetfulness?

_____

_____

_____

_____

3. In what ways are you like the disciples when it comes to temptation?

_____

_____

_____

_____

Today's Prayer

Lord, I don't want to be someone who "doesn't get it." Forgive me for forgetting Your faithfulness and doubting Your power to rescue me from temptation. Help me to regularly take time to remember all the ways You are good to me.

---

1. Warren W. Wiersbe, *The Bible Exposition Commentary* (Wheaton, IL: Victor Books, 1996), 137.

6

DAY SIX
Strength in Our Weakness

Therefore I take pleasure in infirmities, in reproaches, in necessities, in persecutions, in distresses for Christ's sake: for when I am weak, then am I strong.—2 CORINTHIANS 12:10

We all have days when we feel weak, when we are reminded through hardship or failure that we cannot conquer the trials and temptations of life on our own. Thankfully, the Bible is full of stories showing us how God can use ordinary people to demonstrate His extraordinary ability to save us. In Hebrews 11:32–34, we read:

> *And what shall I more say? for the time would fail me to tell of Gedeon, and of Barak, and of Samson, and of Jephthae; of David also, and Samuel, and of the prophets: Who through faith subdued kingdoms, wrought righteousness, obtained promises, stopped the mouths of lions. Quenched the violence of fire, escaped the edge of the sword, out of weakness were made strong, waxed valiant in fight, turned to flight the armies of the aliens.*

Stop trusting in your own strength. Turn instead to God, who is a master at using our weakness for our good and His glory.

Study Time

Read Judges 16, and answer the following questions in the space provided.

1. How was Samson overconfident in his strength?

    _____
    _____
    _____
    _____

2. What does Samson's disobedience in revealing the secret of his strength reveal about him?

    _____
    _____
    _____
    _____

3. Only when he was physically at his weakest was Samson able to do the greatest work he'd ever done (v. 30). What lesson is in this for you?

    _____
    _____
    _____
    _____

Today's Prayer

God, use my life in times of weakness to testify to others of Your great strength. Help me to trust You rather than myself, because You will never fail me.

7
DAY SEVEN
This Is My Story

Come, see a man, which told me all things that ever I did: is not this the Christ?—JOHN 4:29

The power of a story to influence others is well known. Research suggests that the best way to ensure our words are remembered is not to give a list of facts, but to weave knowledge into a story. Perhaps this is one reason the Bible is filled with stories of how God so loved us and continues to show His love daily. Never doubt that your personal account of coming to know God through saving faith can be a powerful influence in someone else's life. Don't keep that story to yourself; tell it to everyone you know.

Study Time

Read John 4:5–30, and answer the following questions in the space provided.

1. Why was the woman of Samaria someone who may have had an interesting influence?

_____

_____

_____

_____

2. What was the result of her sharing her story of meeting Christ?

_____

_____

_____

_____

3. How could your story of trusting God in faith impact others around you? How do you learn more about God by sharing your story?

_____

_____

_____

_____

Today's Prayer

Lord, thank You for loving me and for the gift of story. Give me courage to use my story to reach others for Your kingdom.

What is your story of meeting Christ? Write it down, along with a few ideas of people in your life who could be helped by hearing it.

1
DAY ONE
Warning: Rocks Ahead

Watch and pray, that ye enter not into temptation: the spirit indeed is willing, but the flesh is weak.—MATTHEW 26:41

The mountains of Colorado are among the most beautiful in America, but they pose a threat of injury or death to hundreds of people every year: rock slides. In fact, according to the Colorado Geological Survey, people are more likely to be hit by falling rocks than injured in a highway accident.[1] Yet, while large signs are consistently posted to indicate areas susceptible to falling rocks, they are among the least heeded of all road warning signs because people just don't believe it will happen to them.

What warning signs are you ignoring in your life?

Study Time
Read James 1:5–18, and answer the following questions in the space provided.

1. What is James's warning about our faith in times of temptation (v. 6–8)?

_____

_____

_____

_____

2. According to verses 13–14, how can temptation end?

_____

_____

_____

_____

3. Why do you think James gives a contrast between temptation
    and the gifts of God (v. 17)?

_____

_____

_____

_____

Today's Prayer

*God, give me wisdom and discernment so I may be able to better
heed the warning signs You place in my life. Help me to remember
that Your warnings are given from love because You want the best
for me.*

A great way to ensure against ignoring a warning sign is to
have a friend who knows your struggles and can help watch
your back. Find someone who can encourage you and hold
you accountable in times of temptation.

---

1. Jon White and T.C. Wait, "Rockfall in Colorado," Rock Talk 11, no. 2
    (2008): 2.

2
DAY TWO
Building Endurance

Blessed is the man that endureth temptation: for when he is tried, he shall receive the crown of life, which the Lord hath promised to them that love him.—JAMES 1:12

According to health and fitness experts, a few of the common mistakes people make when trying to achieve an exercise goal are neglecting high-intensity training, relying on routine rather than switching up a workout, and underestimating the power of a good night's rest.[1] Similarly, many Christians don't understand that if we want to realize the goal of spiritual maturity and increased closeness to Christ, we must build endurance through embracing our trials and temptation, relying on God's strength, and resting in the promises found in His Word to see us victoriously through. Remember: to get the result you want in your spiritual life, a little endurance will go a long way.

Study Time

Read James 1:1–4, and answer the following questions in the space provided.

1. What is the motivation for joy in temptation?

_____

_____

_____

_____

2. What do we need in the times when our faith is tested?

_____

_____

_____

_____

3. Why do you think trials and temptations often come together? Which typically comes first in your life?

_____

_____

_____

_____

Today's Prayer

Jesus, give me patience in times of trial and temptation. Show me how You can use them for Your glory and bring me closer to You.

1. Amby Burfoot, "Boost Your Endurance," Runner's World, September 3, 2003, http://www.runnersworld.com/running-tips/boost-your-endurance?page=single, (accessed August 1, 2014).

3
DAY THREE
When No One's Looking

And be not conformed to this world: but be ye transformed by the renewing of your mind, that ye may prove what is that good, and acceptable, and perfect will of God.—ROMANS 12:2

Merriam-Webster defines *integrity* as "firm adherence to a code of especially moral or artistic values,"[1] but the meaning goes deeper than that. Barbara Killinger wrote, "Integrity is a personal choice, an **uncompromising and predictably consistent** commitment to honour moral, ethical, spiritual and artistic values and principles."[2] Integrity means your beliefs and your actions are the same no matter who is watching and you can be trusted to do right even if no one would ever know what you did.

Who are you when no one is looking? If you are someone who is consistently uncompromising and predictable in God-honoring habits, you will pass the test of temptation every time.

Study Time
Read Genesis 39:3–12, and answer the following questions in the space provided.

1. What does the blessing of Joseph in verses 3–5 tell us about temptation?

   _____

   _____

_____

_____

2. What can we learn from Joseph's fleeing in verse 12?

_____

_____

_____

_____

3. In what areas in your life do you struggle because you are not the same person in private as you are in public?

_____

_____

_____

_____

Today's Prayer

Lord, I can hide nothing from You—You see all my faults, and yet You love me. I want to be a person of integrity. Help me ask for Your help and guidance rather than try to pretend I don't struggle with temptation.

1. Merriam-Webster Online, "Integrity," www.merriam-webster.com/dictionary/integrity, (accessed August 1, 2014).
2. Barbara Killinger, "Integrity," Stanford Encyclopedia of Philosophy, January 25, 2013, http://plato.stanford.edu/entries/integrity/, (accessed August 1, 2014).

4
DAY FOUR
Wise Up

Wisdom is the principal thing; therefore get wisdom: and with all thy getting get understanding.—PROVERBS 4:7

If you've ever suspected you might be a genius—or at least smarter than most people you know—these statistics might be a bit discouraging. Research into IQ scores suggests more than half the people in the world have merely average intelligence, while 2.5 percent have superior intelligence, and a tiny 0.5 percent of all the world's population would be considered geniuses.

We don't know whether King Solomon was part of this top 3 percent of the world's smartest people. But his God-given insights into the world and the heart of man led to some of the best advice we'll ever hear about temptation. So take some lessons from the wisest man to have ever lived and learn how wisdom can direct our choices in times of trial.

Study Time

Read Ecclesiastes 1:12–18, and answer the following questions in the space provided.

1. What did Solomon learn in all of his pursuits?

_____

_____

_____

_____

2. What things do you tend to pursue or spend time doing that are "*vain*" or useless in God's big picture?

_____

_____

_____

_____

3. What things that add value to your walk with God should you start pursuing instead?

_____

_____

_____

_____

Today's Prayer

Lord, I don't want to waste a moment of the time I have on Earth doing things that won't glorify You. Show me how I can more wisely use my life in serving You.

5
DAY FIVE
Saved to Serve

And whosoever will be chief among you, let him be your servant: Even as the Son of man came not to be ministered unto, but to minister, and to give his life a ransom for many. —MATTHEW 20:27–28

It has been said that everyone serves something. Most people serve themselves and their own ambitions in order to get money, influence, or love. But the life of the Christian demands the contrary. It demands the commitment to always seek to fulfill God's purpose because He alone is worthy of our service.

...Worthy is the Lamb that was slain to receive power, and riches, and wisdom, and strength, and honour, and glory, and blessing.—REVELATION 5:12

Study Time

Read Romans 6:1–19, and answer the following questions in the space provided.

1. What is the error in thinking "If God's forgiveness is complete, I can do whatever I want"?

_____

_____

_____

_____

2. What did Paul mean by *"ye were the servants of sin"*?

_____

_____

_____

_____

3. What is the power of yielding (v. 19)? Do your actions indicate your life is yielded to sin or to righteousness?

_____

_____

_____

_____

Today's Prayer

Make me a servant to Your will and purpose, Lord. A life of service to You is the best there is.

6
DAY SIX
No Regrets

Be not deceived; God is not mocked: for whatsoever a man soweth, that shall he also reap. For he that soweth to his flesh shall of the flesh reap corruption; but he that soweth to the Spirit shall of the Spirit reap life everlasting.—GALATIANS 6:7–8

Rodger Cromie, director of Northern Ireland Prison Service, knows the face of regret—he sees it every day in the nearly two hundred inmates he's responsible for. In a 2008 interview he observed that when prisoners successfully transition to a path of rehabilitation, their progress comes with the price of regret: "There is a period when a prisoner has to come to terms with the shock that they have been sentenced, what they have been sentenced to, and overcoming the shock of what he or she has done."[1]

When we serve our own desires rather than the things of God, we're in danger of being like those prisoners: trapped in the consequences of our sin and full of regret for what we've done. Refuse to live in such a way that you'll have regrets.

Study Time
Read Romans 6:20–23, and answer the following questions in the space provided.

1. Notice the past tense of verse 20. What does this mean about being a follower of Jesus?

_____

_____

_____

_____

2. What is the result of choosing to serve sin?

_____

_____

_____

_____

3. How have wrong choices in your past led you to experience regret? How are you living differently now?

_____

_____

_____

_____

Today's Prayer

Thank You, God, for the grace of salvation that allows a slave of sin to become a child of God. Help me to live for You so that I may be free of regret.

---

1. "'Many criminals show regret over what they have done,'" News Letter, December 14, 2008, http://www.newsletter.co.uk/news/regional/many-criminals-show-regret-over-what-they-have-done-1-1879376, (accessed August 1, 2014).

7
DAY SEVEN
The Blessing of Correction

Behold, happy is the man whom God correcteth: therefore despise not thou the chastening of the Almighty:—JOB 5:17

The Lord deals with His children much like we as parents or teachers deal with our children. In order to see growth in their lives, sometimes it is necessary to first correct wrong behaviors or attitudes before we show them the right approach. In the same way, many times the Lord in His mercy will chasten us so that He can teach us how to follow Him. Never despair when these times come into your life. Although He may first correct you when you have fallen down, He will always help you back up.

Study Time

Read Psalm 94:11–15, and answer the following questions in the space provided.

1. What does the Lord's knowledge teach us about Him? What does it teach us about ourselves?

    _____

    _____

    _____

    _____

2. What do verses 14 and 18 teach us about the mercy of God?

_____

_____

_____

_____

3. What are the benefits of chastening (vv. 12–13)? How do you know this to be true from your own experiences?

_____

_____

_____

_____

Today's Prayer

Thank You for loving me enough to correct me when I stray, Lord.
Thank You for never leaving me even when I fall.

Memorize Psalm 94:17–19.

1
DAY ONE
Changed

Not by works of righteousness which we have done, but according to his mercy he saved us, by the washing of regeneration, and renewing of the Holy Ghost; Which he shed on us abundantly through Jesus Christ our Saviour;—TITUS 3:5–6

In 2009, thanks to a program offered at San Jose State University, Armando Aguilar was finally able to escape the shadow of his past. Six years after serving his time in prison for burglary and drug possession, Aguilar had turned his life around and even graduated from college with certification to work as a substance abuse counselor—but his history made him virtually unemployable. With the help of the SJSU program, however, his record was wiped clean. One administrator of the program said, "By the time [our clients] get to us, they've changed their lives completely. They deserve a chance to prove it, and to be able to give back to their families and communities."[1]

God has a felony record-expunging program, too: His Son, Jesus Christ. After we place our faith in Him, we will be forever changed.

Study Time

Read Psalm 119:9–13, and answer the following questions in the space provided.

1. How can we be cleansed through the Word of God?

_____

_____

_____

_____

2. According to verse 13, what will happen when we know God's Word?

_____

_____

_____

_____

3. What type of commitment does it take to follow God's Word in our daily living? What things in your life have gotten in the way of making this commitment?

_____

_____

_____

_____

Today's Prayer

Lord, I want my life to reflect the complete transformation that took place in my soul the moment I trusted You for salvation. Help me commit to following Your Word daily so I can better serve You and Your people.

---

1. Mark Gomez, "SJSU program gives reformed criminals a second chance," San Jose Mercury News, May, 22, 2014, http://www.mercurynews.com/bay-area-news/ci_25817690/sjsu-program-gives-reformed-criminals-second-chance, (accessed August 1, 2014).

2

DAY TWO
Neat Freak

Purge me with hyssop, and I shall be clean: wash me, and I shall be whiter than snow.—PSALM 51:7

Is your bathroom floor so spotless someone could eat dinner from it? Does every item in your pantry have a preordained place? How do you feel about hand sanitizer? If you're someone who finds joy or peace in keeping things tidy, our society has developed a few choice terms of endearment to describe how wonderful you are: neat/clean freak, obsessive-compulsive, just plain "weird"...the list goes on.

But if we're children of God, we all should be preoccupied with being clean—spiritually clean, that is. And there's only one way to go about that sort of cleansing: allowing God's Word to shine a spotlight on the sin in our lives, confessing it to God, and turning from it completely.

Study Time

Read Psalm 51:1–10, and answer the following questions in the space provided.

1. What are the "inward parts" of verse 6?

_____

_____

_____

_____

2. Is it in our power to cleanse ourselves? Explain your answer.

_____

_____

_____

_____

3. What is the public or visible evidence of a clean heart and right spirit (verse 10)?

_____

_____

_____

_____

Today's Prayer

Search me, O God, and know my heart (Psalm 139:23). Cleanse me of sin and show me how to live righteously so that You may be glorified through me.

Create a chore list for cleaning up your life. Include those thoughts, attitudes, and behaviors that you must purge; and the thoughts, attitudes, and behaviors you need to add into your life.

3
DAY THREE
The Clean Servant

Blessed are the undefiled in the way, who walk in the law of the Lord. Blessed are they that keep his testimonies, and that seek him with the whole heart. They also do no iniquity: they walk in his ways.—Psalm 119:1–3

During His time on earth, Jesus told several parables, many of which involved characters who were responsible to a master or employer for certain tasks. From these and other instructions in the Bible we get a pretty good idea of what's required of anyone who would be a servant of Jesus Christ. We must be willing and responsible stewards of things He entrusts to our care. We must be faithful to do what He calls us to do. We must be patient and watchful. But most importantly, we must be clean. Paul instructed, "...*Let every one that nameth the name of Christ depart from iniquity. But in a great house there are not only vessels of gold and of silver, but also of wood and of earth; and some to honour, and some to dishonour. If a man therefore purge himself from these, he shall be a vessel unto honour, sanctified, and meet for the master's use, and prepared unto every good work*" (2 Timothy 2:19–21).

Study Time

Read John 13:4–9, and answer the following questions in the space provided.

1. What do Jesus' actions in verses 4–5 teach us about serving?

_____

_____

_____

_____

2. How are we like Peter in his initial response when Christ sought to cleanse him?

_____

_____

_____

_____

3. What do you need to be cleansed of today so you can be prepared for the good works God has called you to?

_____

_____

_____

_____

Today's Prayer

Lord, may I never refuse You when You convict me of my need to be cleansed of sin. Help me to respond quickly and resolutely to rid my life of sin so You can use me however You see fit.

4

DAY FOUR
Are You Plugged In?

So then faith cometh by hearing, and hearing by the word of God.
—ROMANS 10:17

Have you ever used the phrase "as different as night from day"? That's the kind of change the apostle Paul experienced in Acts 9. Previously named Saul, this man was responsible for bringing persecution and death to the early church, but his transformation was so complete that even his name was changed.

The power of God to change us when we trust Him in faith for salvation is unlike anything we've ever known. And this is the same power that is accessible to us when we face temptation. How are you using your power source?

Study Time

Read Acts 9:1–27, and answer the following questions in the space provided.

1. How does Paul's experience in verses 4–18 align with what we read above in Romans 10:17?

    _____

    _____

    _____

    _____

2. Is true faith ever possible apart from God's Word? What in Paul's story would indicate your belief?

_____

_____

_____

_____

3. How did God provide escape from temptation for Paul? How does He provide it for You?

_____

_____

_____

_____

Today's Prayer

Lord, thank You for Your power that changes completely those who trust You for salvation. Help me to trust You in temptation to provide for me just as You did for Paul.

Memorize Romans 10:17.

5

DAY FIVE
I Wanna Be Like ~~Mike~~ David

Blessed are they that keep his testimonies, and that seek him with the whole heart. They also do no iniquity: they walk in his ways.
—PSALM 119:2–3

Some may well wonder why David was called a man after God's own heart (Acts 13:22), especially considering that he gave in to temptations that seem worse than most of our own. After all, he was an adulterer and a murderer (2 Samuel 11).

But David was also a man of absolute faith in God and a lover of God's law. He truly had an understanding of who God is, which is reflected in his psalms of praise as well as his pleas for God's intervention and direction. Lastly, David was truly repentant for his sin and desired nothing more wholeheartedly than to have his relationship with his God restored when he went astray.

Forget the celebrities or great minds of our culture. If we want to make a difference in our world for God, we'll seek to be more like David—because he spent his life seeking to be more like God.

Study Time

Read Psalm 25:4–15, and answer the following questions in the space provided.

1. Why isn't it enough to just read the Bible?

    _____

    _____

    _____

    _____

2. Why do you think David made the distinction that he wanted to be led in "*thy*" truth (verse 5)?

    _____

    _____

    _____

    _____

3. What does it mean to have our eyes "*ever toward the LORD*" (verse 15)? Where is your gaze?

    _____

    _____

    _____

    _____

Today's Prayer

God, You placed examples like David in the Bible to show me how to live. Help me to learn from the lessons You taught him so that I, too, may be someone after Your own heart.

6

DAY SIX

You Can Run...and You Can Hide

Thou art my hiding place; thou shalt preserve me from trouble; thou shalt compass me about with songs of deliverance. Selah.
—PSALM 32:7

We may speak of what can happen when we don't flee temptation, but there are few biblical examples of such that are so vivid as what we find in the story of Jonah. Called by God to go to Nineveh, Jonah instead set sail for Tarshish, but God caught up with him and in love showed him the error of his ways.

If only Christians would flee *from* temptation with the same unforgettable passion that Jonah ran *to* it! If we did, we'd soon find that God is more than able to give us what we need to live for Him through temptation and emerge stronger than ever.

Study Time

Read Psalm 18:30–49, and answer the following questions in the space provided.

1. David writes of several things he learned as a result of trusting God. What are they?

_____

_____

_____

_____

2. How does knowing God's Word is "*tried*" and proven help us run from temptations instead of toward them?

_____

_____

_____

_____

Today's Prayer

Lord, teach me to run to You instead of away from You and toward my own desires. Lead and protect me through temptation unto victory, as You did for David.

7
DAY SEVEN
Power from Within

Let the word of Christ dwell in you richly in all wisdom; teaching and admonishing one another in psalms and hymns and spiritual songs, singing with grace in your hearts to the Lord. And whatsoever ye do in word or deed, do all in the name of the Lord Jesus, giving thanks to God and the Father by him.—COLOSSIANS 3:16–17

On October 15, 1997, David Huxley strapped a harness around his upper torso and attached it to a steel cable some fifteen yards long. The other end of the steel cable was attached to the front-wheel strut of a 747 jetliner that weighed 187 tons. With his tennis shoes firmly planted on the runway, Huxley leaned forward, pulled with all his might, and began moving the jetliner down the runway. In fact, he pulled the 747 one hundred yards in one minute and twenty-one seconds.[1]

Living a victorious Christian life is much like that 747 jetliner. Although Huxley was able to pull it a short distance, it is impossible to pull an airplane any real distance without using its engines. Even so, we may be able to briefly resist temptation in the strength of our willpower, but without the power of God's Spirit within, we'll run out of strength.

Thankfully, we do have the power of Christ within—a power strong enough to deliver us in temptation as we stand firm in His Word!

Study Time

Read Psalm 107:19, and answer the following questions in the space provided.

1. Where should our hope be found?

_____

_____

_____

_____

2. What steps did the psalmist take so that the influence of God's Word was the focus of his life?

_____

_____

_____

_____

3. What has God taught you about Himself through this study?

_____

_____

_____

_____

Today's Prayer

Lord, give me the wisdom and grace to trust in Your Word despite the struggles I'm facing and despite what the world may say or think. Give me the courage to stand in Your power, unafraid of any temptation, knowing the only One with a hold on my life is You.

Novelist Tim O'Brien once said, "The thing about remembering is that you don't forget." Be intentional about your plan to remember the things you've learned and studied throughout this series. Write down a few of your strategies here, along with today's date, so that you can track your progress as you continue to grow in the Lord.

_____

_____

_____

_____

_____

_____

_____

_____

_____

_____

_____

_____

Date _____

1. Craig Brian Larson, *750 Engaging Illustrations for Preachers, Teachers, and Writers* (Baker Books, 2007), 62.

Saved: The Most Needful Escape

I heard once of two men standing by the road with a sign that read "The End Is Near." As a driver passed right on by them, they waved their arms, frantically signaling that he should stop. But it was to no avail. Pretty soon, they heard a gigantic splash.

"Perhaps," one of the sign-bearers said to the other, "we should have just written 'The Bridge Is Out.'"

We can all be stubborn to or disregard warnings that don't seem relevant to us. There is one warning, however, that we dare not ignore—the warning God has given of the penalty of death and Hell for sin. Some people scoff at the mention of Hell, but Scripture tells us it is a real place—and that God has provided a way of escape.

To understand how to take this—the most-needful escape of life—we must first understand why God gives us this warning.

Recognize your condition

I'll never forget the Sunday I attended church years ago and heard a guest speaker from Arkansas who asked me a question that really bothered me: "Do you know for sure that if you died today, you'd go to Heaven?" The fact was, I really didn't know. I couldn't honestly claim to be sure that God was my Heavenly Father.

You see, I have a problem—and you do, too. The problem that we share is the fact that none of us are perfect. We are all sinners, as is so clearly spelled out in Romans 3:10 (*"As it is written, There is none righteous, no, not one"*) and Romans 3:23 (*"For all have sinned, and come short of the glory of God"*).

No one had to teach us how to sin; we were just born that way. We received no training to be able to lie, think wrong thoughts, or even be selfish. This is evident in the story of the brother and sister who were playing on a kiddie horse ride outside a grocery store. The boy, irritated that he had to share the ride with his sister, said, "You know, if one of us would get off, there would be more room for me."

Understanding we are sinners is really not news to us. We all know that we aren't perfect and don't measure up to God's standards. But more than that, the Bible is clear that there is a penalty for being a sinner: *"For the wages of sin is death; but the gift of God is eternal life through Jesus Christ our Lord"* (Romans 6:23).

God is perfect and holy. We are imperfect sinners. This is where the breach comes. We are separated from God by our sin, and God tells us the wages—the payment—for sin is eternal separation from God. Revelation 20:14 refers to this as *"the second death"*: *"And death and hell were cast into the lake of fire. This is the second death."*

Religion and good works are not the answer

Religions try to create their own ways to God. Their systems may seem logical, but they cannot bridge the gap created by our sin. Proverbs 14:12 says, *"There is a way which seemeth right unto a man, but the end thereof are the ways of death."* In other words, our thoughts and ways are not what matter. God's Word, the Bible, provides true answers of grace and forgiveness. As we saw a moment ago, Ephesians 2:8–9 says, *"For by grace are ye saved through faith; and that not of yourselves: it is the gift of God: Not of works, lest any man should boast."*

The good news—Jesus Christ provides the way

Through His death on the cross, Jesus Christ paid for our sins. Although the *"wages of sin is death,"* Romans 5:8 tells us, *"But God commendeth* [meaning proved or demonstrated] *his love toward us, in that, while we were yet sinners, Christ died for us."* Very simply, Jesus paid our wage of sin when He died on the cross.

Even though we were lost and separated from God, He loved us. And because He is love, God sent His Son to die on the cross and rise from the dead three days later. John 3:16 explains *"For God so loved the world, that he gave his only begotten Son, that whosoever believeth in him should not perish, but have everlasting life."*

Through the death and resurrection of Jesus, He became the payment for our sin. Now, we do not have to pay for our sin ourselves. He sacrificially provided the way of escape.

Believe and receive Christ

Just because a gift has been purchased and offered does not mean the person for whom it was intended now owns it. Jesus purchased our salvation when He died for our sins, and He offers us full forgiveness based on what He did for us. But we must receive His offered gift to have eternal life. We must place our full trust in Jesus Christ alone for forgiveness and eternal life. We must stop trusting ourselves, our works, or our religions, and place our full trust in Jesus Christ alone.

In Romans 10:13 the Bible says, *"For whosoever shall call upon the name of the Lord shall be saved."*

Saved. Saved from the penalty of sin, saved from eternal death in Hell, saved into a real relationship with God.

That is a promise directly from God that if you will pray to Him, confess that you are a sinner, ask Him to forgive your sins, and turn to Him alone to be your Saviour; He will save you and give you the free gift of eternal life. You can make that decision today by praying from your heart, something like this:

> Dear God, I know that I am separated from You because of sin. I confess that in my sin, I cannot save myself. Right now, I turn to You alone to be my Saviour. I ask You to save me from the penalty of my sin, and I trust You to provide eternal life for me.
> —Amen

You'll never regret that decision! If you have just trusted Christ, I would love to know about your decision and give you a gift Bible and some other materials to help you learn more about that new relationship! Please send an email to escape@strivingtogether.com, and let me know today!

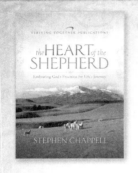

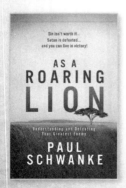

Visit us online

strivingtogether.com

wcbc.edu